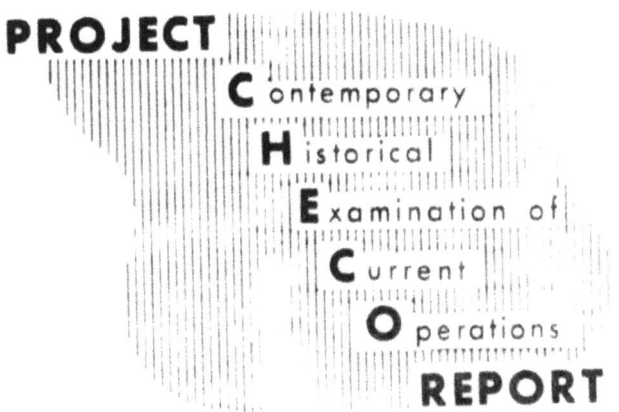

# PROJECT CHECO REPORT
**C**ontemporary **H**istorical **E**xamination of **C**urrent **O**perations

# THE CAMBODIAN CAMPAIGN (U)
# 29 APRIL - 30 JUNE 1970

## 1 SEPTEMBER 1970

### HQ PACAF
Directorate, Tactical Evaluation
CHECO Division

> Prepared by:
> MAJOR D. I. FOLKMAN, Jr.
> & MAJOR P. D. CAINE
> Project CHECO 7th AF, DOAC

PROJECT CHECO REPORTS

The counterinsurgency and unconventional warfare environment of Southeast Asia has resulted in the employment of USAF airpower to meet a multitude of requirements. The varied applications of airpower have involved the full spectrum of USAF aerospace vehicles, support equipment, and manpower. As a result, there has been an accumulation of operational data and experiences that, as a priority, must be collected, documented, and analyzed as to current and future impact upon USAF policies, concepts, and doctrine.

Fortunately, the value of collecting and documenting our SEA experiences was recognized at an early date. In 1962, Hq USAF directed CINCPACAF to establish an activity that would be primarily responsive to Air Staff requirements and direction, and would provide timely and analytical studies of USAF combat operations in SEA.

Project CHECO, an acronym for Contemporary Historical Examination of Current Operations, was established to meet this Air Staff requirement. Managed by Hq PACAF, with elements at Hq 7AF and 7AF/13AF, Project CHECO provides a scholarly, "on-going" historical examination, documentation, and reporting on USAF policies, concepts, and doctrine in PACOM. This CHECO report is part of the overall documentation and examination which is being accomplished. Along with the other CHECO publications, this is an authentic source for an assessment of the effectiveness of USAF airpower in PACOM.

ROLAND K. CAMPBELL, Major General, USAF
Chief of Staff

REPLY TO
ATTN OF: DOVD

1 September 1970

SUBJECT: Project CHECO Report, "The Cambodian Campaign,
29 April to 30 June 1970" (U)

TO: SEE DISTRIBUTION PAGE

1. Attached is a TOP SECRET NOFORN document. It shall be transported, stored, safeguarded, and accounted for in accordance with applicable security directives. Each page is marked according to its contents. The information contained in this document will not be disclosed to foreign nationals or their representatives. Retain or destroy in accordance with AFR 205-1. Do not return.

2. Reproduction of this document in whole or in part is prohibited except with the permission of the office of origin.

3. This letter does not contain classified information and may be declassified if attachment is removed from it.

FOR THE COMMANDER IN CHIEF

MAURICE L. GRIFFITH, Colonel, USAF
Chief, CHECO Division
Directorate, Tactical Evaluation
DCS/Operations

1 Atch
Proj CHECO Rprt (TS/NF),
1 Sep 70

## DISTRIBUTION LIST

1. SECRETARY OF THE AIR FORCE

    a. SAFAA . . . . . . . 1(1)
    b. SAFLL . . . . . . . 1(2)
    c. SAFOI . . . . . . . 2(3,4)

2. HEADQUARTERS USAF

    a. AFNB . . . . . . . . 1(5)

    b. AFCCS
        (1) AFCCSSA . . . . 1(6)
        (2) AFCVC . . . . . 1(7)
        (3) AFCAV . . . . . 1(8)
        (4) AFCHO . . . . . 2(9,10)

    c. AFCSA
        (1) AFCSAG . . . . . 1(11)
        (2) AFCSAMI . . . . 1(12)

    d. AFOA . . . . . . . . 2(13,14)

    e. AFIGO
        (1) OSIUAM . . . . . 3(15-17)
        (2) IGS . . . . . . 1(18)

    f. AFSG . . . . . . . . 1(19)

    g. AFNIATC . . . . . . 5(20-24)

    h. AFAAC . . . . . . . 1(25)
        (1) AFACMI . . . . . 1(26)

    i. AFODC
        (1) AFPRC . . . . . 1(27)
        (2) AFPRE . . . . . 1(28)
        (3) AFPRM . . . . . 1(29)

    j. AFPDC
        (1) AFDPXPS . . . . 1(30)
        (2) AFDPMD . . . . . 1(31)
        (3) AFDPW . . . . . 1(32)

    k. AF/RD . . . . . . . 1(33)
        (1) AFRDP . . . . . 1(34)
        (2) AFRDQ . . . . . 1(35)
        (3) AFRDQRC . . . . 1(36)
        (4) AFRDR . . . . . 1(37)

    l. AFSDC
        (1) AFSLP . . . . . 1(38)
        (2) AFSME . . . . . 1(39)
        (3) AFSMS . . . . . 1(40)
        (4) AFSPD . . . . . 1(41)
        (5) AFSSS . . . . . 1(42)
        (6) AFSTP . . . . . 1(43)

    m. AFTAC . . . . . . . 1(44)

    n. AFXO . . . . . . . . 1(45)
        (1) AFXOD . . . . . 1(46)
        (2) AFXODC . . . . 1(47)
        (3) AFXODD . . . . 1(48)
        (4) AFXODL . . . . 1(49)
        (5) AFXOOAB . . . . 1(50)
        (6) AFXOSL . . . . 1(51)
        (7) AFXOOSN . . . . 1(52)
        (8) AFXOOSO . . . . 1(53)
        (9) AFXOOSS . . . . 1(54)
        (10) AFXOOSV . . . . 1(55)
        (11) AFXOOTR . . . . 1(56)
        (12) AFXOOTW . . . . 1(57)
        (13) AFXOOTZ . . . . 1(58)
        (14) AFXOOCY . . . . 1(59)
        (15) AF/XOX . . . . 6(60-65)
        (16) AFXOXXG . . . . 3(66-68)

3. MAJOR COMMAND

   a. TAC

      (1) HEADQUARTERS
          (a) DO . . . . . . . . . 1(69)
          (b) DPL . . . . . . . . 2(70,71)
          (c) DOCC . . . . . . . . 1(72)
          (d) DREA . . . . . . . . 1(73)
          (e) DIO . . . . . . . . 1(74)

   b. SAC

      (1) HEADQUARTERS
          (a) DOPL . . . . . . . . 1(75)
          (b) XPX . . . . . . . . 1(76)
          (c) DM . . . . . . . . . 1(77)
          (d) DI . . . . . . . . . 1(78)
          (e) OA . . . . . . . . . 1(79)
          (f) HO . . . . . . . . . 1(80)

   c. MAC

      (1) HEADQUARTERS
          (a) DOI . . . . . . . . 1(81)
          (b) DOO . . . . . . . . 1(82)
          (c) MACHO . . . . . . . 1(83)
          (d) MACOA . . . . . . . 1(84)

   d. ADC

      (1) HEADQUARTERS
          (a) DO . . . . . . . . . 1(85)
          (b) DOT . . . . . . . . 1(86)
          (c) XPC . . . . . . . . 1(87)

   e. ATC

      (1) HEADQUARTERS
          (a) ATXPP-X . . . . . . 1(88)

   f. AFLC

      (1) HEADQUARTERS
          (a) MCVSS . . . . . . . 1(89)

   i. AAC
      (1) HEADQUARTERS
          (a) ALDOC-A . . . . . . . 1(90)

   j. USAFSO
      (1) HEADQUARTERS
          (a) CSH . . . . . . . . . 1(91)

   k. PACAF
      (1) HEADQUARTERS
          (a) DP . . . . . . . . . 1(92)
          (b) IN . . . . . . . . . 1(93)
          (c) XP . . . . . . . . . 2(94,95)
          (d) CSH . . . . . . . . . 1(96)
          (e) DOVD . . . . . . . . 5(97-101)
          (f) DC . . . . . . . . . 1(102)
          (g) DM . . . . . . . . . 1(103)
          (h) DOVH . . . . . . . . 1(104)

      (2) AIR FORCES
          (a) DOAC . . . . . . . . 2(105,106)

   l. USAFE
      (1) HEADQUARTERS
          (a) DOA . . . . . . . . . 1(107)
          (b) DOLO . . . . . . . . 1(108)
          (c) DOO . . . . . . . . . 1(109)
          (d) XDC . . . . . . . . . 1(110)

4. SEPARATE OPERATING AGENCIES

   a. ACIC(DOP) . . . . . . . . . . 2(111,112)
   b. AFRES(XP) . . . . . . . . . . 2(113,114)
   c. USAFA
      (1) CMT . . . . . . . . . . . 1(115)
      (2) DFH . . . . . . . . . . . 1(116)

   d. AU
      (1) ACSC-SA . . . . . . . . . 1(117)
      (2) AUL(SE)-69-108 . . . . . 1(118)
      (3) ASI(ASD-1) . . . . . . . 1(119)
      (4) ASI(HOA) . . . . . . . . 2(120,121)
   e. AFAFC(CEH) . . . . . . . . . 1(122)
   f. ANALYTIC SERVICES, INC . . . 1(123)

# TABLE OF CONTENTS

| | PAGE |
|---|---|
| FOREWORD | ix |
| SUMMARY | x |
|   Air Support of Ground Forces | xi |
|   Interdiction | xiv |
| CHAPTER I - BACKGROUND | 1 |
| CHAPTER II - AIR SUPPORT OF GROUND FORCES | 8 |
|     Ground Operations | 8 |
|     Air Support | 11 |
|     Air Resources | 26 |
|     Campaign Results | 29 |
| CHAPTER III - INTERDICTION | 34 |
|     Enemy Offensive | 34 |
|     Establishment of Interdiction Campaign | 36 |
|     Target Development | 44 |
|     Operation FREEDOM DEAL | 48 |
|     Expanded Interdiction | 52 |
| CHAPTER IV - AIRLIFT SUPPORT | 60 |
| FOOTNOTES | |
|   Foreword | 61 |
|   Chapter I | 61 |
|   Chapter II | 61 |
|   Chapter III | 63 |
| APPENDIXES | |
|   I. (C) Air Summary, USAF; Air Summary, VNAF | 67 |
|   II. (S) Using Airplanes, with Fig. 1, Air Ground Request Net; Use of Signal Panels | 71 |
|   III. (S) FREEDOM DEAL LOC Status | 76 |
| GLOSSARY | 77 |

FIGURES                                                              Follows Page

1.  (C)  Allied Operations in Cambodia, 29 Apr - 30 Jun 70 ..   x
2.  (C)  Areas of RVN/US Operations in Cambodia ............    x
3.  (C)  VC/NVA Logistic Network Base Areas ................    2
4.  (S)  Cambodian Base Camps - Estimates Prior to
         Operations ........................................    2
5.  (C)  Supply Cache Located in Cambodia ..................    6
6.  (C)  Parrot's Beak, TOAN THANG 42, 29 Apr - 5 May 70 ....   8
7.  (U)  Troops Investigate Ammunition Stockpile ...........   10
8.  (C)  Cambodian Target ..................................   14
9.  (C)  ARC LIGHT Airstrikes ..............................   16
10. (C)  FISHHOOK (TOAN THANG 43) ..........................   16
11. (C)  Airstrikes, TOAN THANG 42 (Parrot's Beak) .........   18
12. (U)  Munitions Concealed in Heavy Undergrowth ..........   18
13. (C)  Airstrikes, TOAN THANG 44; Airstrikes, TOAN THANG
         45/46..............................................   24
14. (C)  Airstrikes, BINH TAY I; Airstrikes, BINH TAY II ....  24
15. (C)  Airstrikes, BINH TAY III; Airstrikes, CUU LONG I ...  24
16. (C)  Airstrikes, CUU LONG II; Airstrikes, CUU LONG III ..  24
17. (C)  Airstrikes - USAF; VNAF ...........................   24
18. (C)  Sortie Distribution ...............................   26
19. (C)  Aircraft Utilization ..............................   26
20. (C)  Weekly Sortie Distribution ........................   26
21. (U)  Helicopter Landing Zone Preparation ...............   28
22. (C)  COMMANDO VAULT Drops ..............................   28
23. (C)  Bomb Damage Assessment by Operation ...............   28
24. (S)  Ordnance Delivered; ARC LIGHT Summary .............   28
25. (C)  Tactical Air Support for Cambodian Operations .....   30
26. (C)  Significant Cambodian Caches ......................   30
27. (C)  Large Cache Complexes .............................   30
28. (C)  City Cache ........................................   30
29. (C)  Rock Island East Cache ............................   30
30. (U)  Munitions Found in Complex ........................   32
31. (U)  Ammunition Stockpile ..............................   32
32. (C)  Enemy Action, 1 May - 30 Jun 70 ...................   34
33. (S)  Proposed Interdiction Area ........................   36
34. (U)  F-4 Airstrike .....................................   36
35. (S)  FREEDOM DEAL; FREEDOM DEAL Extension ..............   40
36. (C)  Initial Cambodian FAC Sectors .....................   40
37. (C)  Reconnaissance of Water LOC .......................   40
38. (S)  Interdiction Target Request Net ...................   42
39. (S)  Reconnaissance Area Authorized, 21 May 70 .........   44
40. (C)  Bridge and Roadcuts Indicated by Reconnaissance ...   44
41. (C)  Major LOCs in FREEDOM DEAL ........................   44
42. (C)  Airstrikes, 30 May 1970 ...........................   46
43. (C)  Airstrikes, 4 June 1970 ...........................   48

vii

| FIGURES | | | Follows Page |
|---|---|---|---|
| 44. | (S) | Category B LOCs | 48 |
| 45. | (S) | MK-36 Seeding Areas | 48 |
| 46. | (C) | Interdiction Airstrike Summary | 50 |
| 47. | (C) | FREEDOM ACTION, FAC VR Sectors | 52 |
| 48. | (S) | Operation FREEDOM ACTION Air Request Net | 54 |
| 49. | (S) | Airstrikes, Cambodian Interdiction Area | 56 |
| 50. | (C) | Expanded Interdiction Strike Concentrations | 56 |
| 51. | (C) | FAC Sectors After 26 June 1970 | 58 |
| 52. | (S) | Total Tons (Cargo and Passengers) | 60 |
| 53. | (S) | Supporting Airfields | 60 |

# FOREWORD

United States and South Vietnamese forces entering Cambodia on 1 May 1970 seriously weakened the enemy posture as they captured large quantities of his supplies and inflicted heavy casualties on Viet Cong/North Vietnamese Army forces operating in Cambodian sanctuaries. This movement of troops supported by airpower is profiled here in "The Cambodian Campaign, 29 April - 30 June 1970," a special CHECO Report, as one of the most significant actions of the Southeast Asia conflict. The quantity of supplies contained in the caches captured in Cambodia during May - June 1970 exceeded the total supplies contained in all the caches captured in RVN for the 15 months from February 1969 through April 1970.[1]

Airpower was employed in two ways in the Cambodian campaign; first, in tactical air support of friendly ground operations and second, in an interdiction campaign. The interdiction campaign consisted of three phases: (1) a period of limited interdiction in northeastern Cambodia; (2) an extension of interdiction in northeastern Cambodia; and (3) a retrenchment back to a limited area.

The establishment and development of the air interdiction campaign and tactical air and ARC LIGHT missions in support of the operations in Cambodia are detailed in this report, along with a statistical summary of airlift operations.

## SUMMARY

After the 18 March 1970 deposal of Prince Norodom Sihanouk, officials in Washington, D.C. and at Military Assistance Command, Vietnam, began considering plans to seize or destroy supplies and facilities in the sanctuary bases that the North Vietnamese maintained in Cambodia adjacent to South Vietnam. These tightly held considerations led to the decision to employ U.S. forces against the storage areas. In Washington, D.C., on 30 April 1970 (morning of 1 May in Vietnam), President Richard M. Nixon announced that U.S. forces had just entered the FISHHOOK area of Cambodia. This operation, under control of II Field Force Vietnam, began in the early morning of 1 May, Vietnam time. The Cambodian government was notified of the impending action just prior to its initiation. South Vietnamese troops had moved into the Parrot's Beak on 29 April, Vietnam time, but no U.S. troops were involved.

In the next two months, 12 different operations spaced along the length of the Cambodian/RVN Border undertook to drive the enemy out of the sanctuaries, destroy or capture his war materials stored there, and disrupt his retraining and reorganization facilities (Fig. 1). Although U.S. ground forces were prohibited from penetrating beyond 30 kilometers from the border, ARVN forces went much deeper, up to 90 kilometers at the city of Kampong Speu (Fig. 2). At the end of June, U.S. forces were withdrawn, while the ARVN continued one of the operations.

ALLIED OPERATIONS IN CAMBODIA, 29 APR - 30 JUN 70

| OPERATION | DATES | COMPOSITION OF FORCE AT MAX STRENGTH | SELECTED OPERATIONAL RESULTS ||||||||||
|---|---|---|---|---|---|---|---|---|---|---|---|---|
| | | | Enemy ||| Captured/Destroyed |||| Friendly ||||
| | | | KIA | POW | Indiv Wpns | Crew Served Weapons | Ammo T | Rice T | KIA GVN | KIA US | WIA GVN | WIA US |
| TOAN THANG 42 III Corps | 29 Apr - con. on 30 Jun | 9794 GVN 1590 US | 2752 | 767 | 1893 | 478 | 360 | 1042 | 283 | 9 | 1290 | 65 |
| TOAN THANG 42 IV Corps | 29 Apr - 6 May | Not Available | 1202 | 0 | 1146 | 174 | 63 | 46 | 67 | 3 | 329 | 5 |
| TOAN THANG 43 | 1 May - 30 Jun | 13400 GVN 8000 US | 3099 | 73 | 4680 | 731 | 316 | 2699 | 149 | 141 | 656 | 863 |
| BINH TAY I | 5 - 25 May | 2463 GVN 8016 US | 276 | 8 | 842 | 37 | 13 | 602 | 16 | 30 | 98 | 72 |
| TOAN THANG 44 | 6 - 14 May | 2700 US | 283 | 12 | 297 | 34 | 4 | 217 | - | 21 | - | 174 |
| TOAN THANG 45 | 6 May - 30 Jun | 10900 US | 1189 | 12 | 3069 | 449 | 804 | 1584 | - | 126 | - | 332 |
| TOAN THANG 46 | 6 May - 30 Jun | 3160 GVN 32 US | 70 | 9 | 325 | 41 | 10 | 79 | 27 | 0 | 147 | 0 |
| TOAN THANG 500/B16/645 | 7 - 11 May | 900 GVN 900 US | Results included under TOAN THANG 42 III Corps |||||||||||
| CUU LONG I | 9 May - 1 Jul | 11696 GVN 2364 US | 1431 | 61 | 2738 | 157 | 23 | 41 | 148 | 6 | 473 | 5 |
| BINH TAY II | 14 - 26 May | 4593 GVN 392 US | 73 | 6 | 476 | 136 | 27 | 89 | 7 | 2 | 34 | 0 |
| CUU LONG II | 16 - 24 May | 10260 GVN 346 US | 613 | 40 | 792 | 84 | 65 | 44 | 36 | 0 | 122 | 0 |
| BINH TAY III | 20 May - 27 Jun | 3615 GVN 272 US | 141 | 1 | 587 | 133 | 40 | 412 | 26 | 0 | 67 | 7 |
| CUU LONG III | 24 May - con. on 30 Jun | 3727 GVN 147 US | 433 | 36 | 3299 | 80 | 40 | 27 | 50 | 0 | 270 | 1 |
| TOTALS | | | 11562 | 1025 | 20074 | 2534 | 1764 | 6879 | 809 | 338 | 3486 | 1524 |

SOURCE: OB Logistics, MACV

FIGURE 1

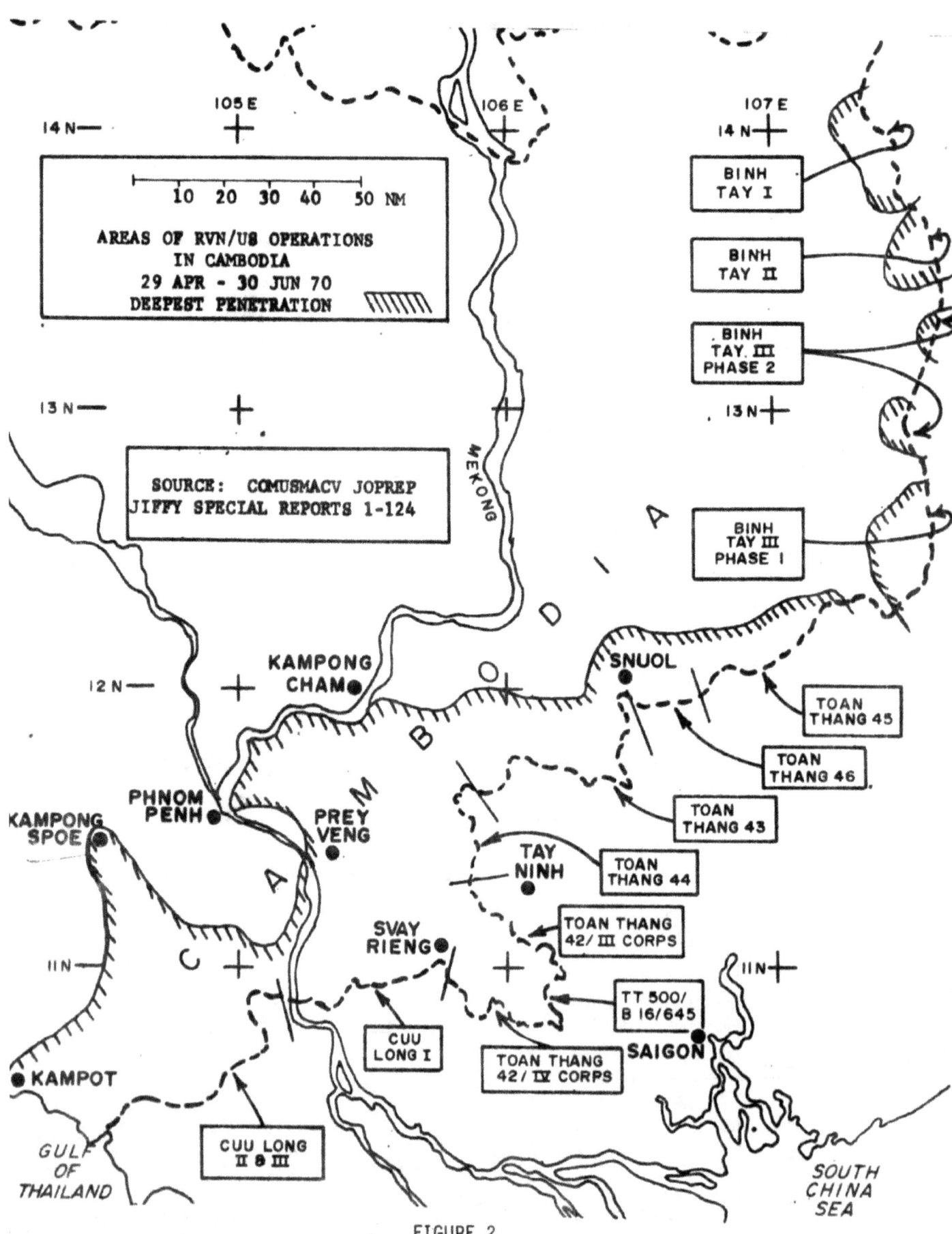

FIGURE 2

Air Support of Ground Forces

The flexible operating capability of the Tactical Air Control System met the requirements of the Cambodian operations with routine efficiency. Even though Seventh Air Force received instructions to begin definitive planning only two days before the ARVN entry into the Parrot's Beak, all tactical air assets were ready on schedule. Forward air controllers and fighter pilots followed normal in-country Rules of Engagement and operating procedures, exercising special care to avoid dropping ordnance on the noncombatant populace.

Because intelligence estimates indicated that heavy enemy resistance could be anticipated, extensive airstrikes were used to suppress enemy resistance prior to combat assaults. Both preplanned and immediate airstrikes supported operations on the ground. Many preplanned airstrikes were diverted from the preplanned targets to support troops in contact and to hit significant targets of opportunity. After the initial assaults, ground forces turned to searching the areas for supplies and evacuating the caches discovered. During this phase, airstrikes were preplanned to furnish air cover and to aid in the discovery and destruction of storage areas.

Although approval for use of Thailand-based forces was received, tactical air support for ground forces came entirely from in-country resources, except for three C-130 flareships deployed from Ubon to Cam Ranh Bay and four A-1 aircraft deployed from Nakhon Phanom to Pleiku and later to Bien Hoa for SAR efforts. The attack sortie rate for in-country forces peaked during the second week in May to 4,336 with the inclusion of 1,936 sorties in Cambodia. USAF fighter aircraft utilization rates increased from pre-Cambodian levels of .75 - .80 sorties per day per aircraft to peak levels of 1.13 for F-4s, 1.38 for A-37s, and 1.44 for F-100s. USAF aircraft flew 5,189 preplanned and 1,675 immediate airstrike sorties as well as 193 gunship and 44 flareship missions. The delivery of 20 COMMANDO VAULT weapons created 16 usable helicopter landing zones. The VNAF flew 2,691 strike sorties and 184 gunship missions. Bomb damage included 926 confirmed and 1,358 probable enemy killed, 6,269 structures and 5,270 bunkers destroyed, and 50 bridges destroyed.

B-52 ARC LIGHT missions flew 653 sorties in support of six of the 12 distinct ground operations in Cambodia. ARC LIGHT airstrikes provided massive firepower for landing zone and objective preparations prior to initial combat assaults. B-52s also struck suspected Central Office of South Vietnam (COSVN) headquarters elements and other enemy locations beyond the 30-kilometer limitation for U.S. ground forces.

Except for some initial heavy contacts in a few areas, the entire ground campaign was characterized by contacts with scattered enemy units. The retreat of the main enemy forces into the interior of Cambodia allowed friendly ground forces to sweep through the base areas with 1,147 killed in action, compared to 11,562 enemy losses. These odds would likely have been much less favorable had tactical air not been available to coerce the enemy from his fortified defenses. The threat as well as the employment of airpower contributed to the ground forces' ability to advance rapidly enough to uncover the numerous caches and then to be able to exploit these caches relatively unmolested.

Among the supplies captured were: (1) rice to feed 37,798 enemy soldiers for one year at reduced ration (1 lb. per day); (2) individual weapons to equip 55 full strength VC Infantry battalions; (3) crew-served weapons to equip 33 full strength VC Infantry battalions; and (4) mortar, rocket, and recoilless rifle rounds to sustain 18,585 enemy attacks by fire. The Logistics Section of the Combined Intelligence Center, Vietnam (CICV) estimated that Allied forces had captured the following percentages of the enemy's food and ammunition stockpiles required by him to operate for a six months' period:

| CATEGORY | AREA | CAPTURED (Tons) | PERCENT OF STOCKPILE |
|---|---|---|---|
| Food | No. II Corps | 683.6 | 65 |
|  | So. II Corps and III, IV Corps | 6,193.0 | 129 |
| Ammo | No. II Corps | 40.6 | 09 |
|  | So. II Corps and III, IV Corps | 1,761.4 | 81 |

CICV concluded that the cross-border operations had severely impaired the enemy's logistic system for southern South Vietnam and he would feel the effects for at least six to eight months as evidenced by more than a six-month stockpile of food being captured in Southern II Corps and III and IV Corps.

## Interdiction

While withdrawing in the face of the Allied advance in eastern Cambodia, the enemy repeatedly attacked key towns on the major lines of communication in the interior of the country; he threatened to isolate Phnom Penh and so fragment the nation that the government could not effectively control it. The towns in northeast Cambodia fell one by one: Kratie on 5-6 May, Stung Treng on 18 May, Siem Pang on 19 May, Lomphat on 31 May, and finally Labansiek and Bakiev were evacuated by the government on 23-25 June 1970 with the aid of USAF transports and fighter protection. This gave the communists control of the entire northeastern section of Cambodia.

In response to the Secretary of Defense, the JCS outlined a plan for an interdiction campaign in northeast Cambodia similar to the STEEL TIGER operation in southern Laos and forwarded it to the Military Assistance Command, Vietnam (MACV) on 16 May 1970. The MACV reply to the Joint Chiefs of Staff (JCS) noted that because there was neither an identified enemy line of communications (LOC) network nor a corresponding logistics flow in northeast Cambodia, the initial requirements for tactical air beyond 30 kilometers would be to support Vietnamese and Cambodian ground units with some interdiction. Since existing authorizations precluded such actions, a plan was developed for air interdiction of lucrative targets developed through reconnaissance.

After being directed to implement the plan, Seventh Air Force activated a Tactical Air Control Party at Pleiku and divided the interdiction area into forward air controller/visual reconnaissance (FAC/VR) sectors. Forward air controllers flying OV-10s and O-2s, and fighter pilots qualified as FACs flying F-4s and A-37s began visual reconnaissance between 25 and 29 May.

Cambodian, Vietnamese, and MACV representatives met on 29 May and established Rules of Engagement similar to those for in-country operations including the provision that all targets had to be validated by the Cambodians. On 4 June 1970, two Cambodian Air Force officers joined the Tactical Air Control Center (TACC) at Tan Son Nhut to validate targets, and three went to Pleiku to fly as observers and to validate targets. In addition, the rules allowed motorized vehicle or boat traffic to be struck on certain LOCs after the populace had received warning.

The lack of an extensive intelligence file on Cambodia created an initial targeting problem. On 21 May, an Intelligence Task Force was organized at Headquarters Seventh Air Force for targeting in Cambodia. Also on 21 May, Seventh Air Force received authority to reconnoiter Cambodia east of the Mekong plus some areas to the west. Airborne Radio Direction Finding (ARDF) activities were extended on 26 May. On 30 May, six targets were struck, inaugurating the interdiction campaign.

The FREEDOM DEAL Operations Order of 6 June stated the interdiction mission: to maintain surveillance of enemy activities in Cambodia, east of the Mekong River and to attack these activities as necessary to protect U.S. forces in the Republic of Vietnam. Daily interdiction sorties began on 4 June. MK36 mines were sown in the Se Kong and Se San Rivers to curtail supply movements.

On 9 June, the JCS authorized tactical reconnaissance in all of Cambodia on a recurring basis. Reconnaissance sorties over Cambodia increased from 315 in May to 324 for the first 20 days of June. An important part of the reconnaissance effort was to photograph national shrines, monuments, and cultural sites. These photographs were sent to FACs, gunship, and strike units flying in Cambodia to assure the protection of these historic areas.

During the period of 1-20 June 1970, tactical aircraft flew 414 preplanned and 224 immediate sorties in the interdiction campaign. After 7 June, the target emphasis shifted from the LOC complex to the area around Lomphat, Labansiek, and Bakiev where it remained for the remainder of the campaign.

The absence of an organized enemy resupply network within the interdiction area became increasingly apparent as the campaign progressed. In addition, concern that loss of major population centers would undermine the Cambodian Government indicated that interdiction should be applied in its broadest sense to protect major Cambodian positions. A JCS message of 17 June became the authority for an expanded interdiction campaign throughout Cambodia called FREEDOM ACTION.

Seventh Air Force divided that part of Cambodia, outside the FREEDOM DEAL area, into six sectors to be covered by FACs based in Thailand

and Vietnam. Prospective targets obtained from monitoring LOCs, major towns, and provincial capitals for possible enemy activity were reported to the TACC for validation and possible strike. Communications ran through the Vietnamese Air Force Direct Air Control Center at Phnom Penh to the TACC at Tan Son Nhut. Backup communications for immediate airstrikes were available through III DASC in South Vietnam. Instructions on how to use air support were distributed to Cambodian ground units and USAF French speaking officers flew with U.S. FACs to facilitate communications.

On 20 June, interdiction sorties struck known enemy locations around Kampong Thom. During the ten days of the expanded interdiction effort, 226 sorties were flown outside the limits of the FREEDOM DEAL area.

On 30 June, the area of operations for the interdiction campaign was limited to the FREEDOM DEAL area plus a small southern extension. Within the southern extension, strikes were authorized on only highly lucrative targets that posed a substantial threat to Allied forces.

The establishment of interdiction operations in northeastern Cambodia compounded the enemy resupply problems. Any enemy effort to develop a LOC system in Cambodia would be costly.

# CHAPTER I

## BACKGROUND

More than two-thirds of the population of the Republic of Vietnam (RVN) live in the southern third of the country, III and IV Corps Tactical Zones (CTZs) and the Capital Military District (CMD) surrounding Saigon. Because the war is really a battle for control of the population, the largest Viet Cong/North Vietnam Army (VC/NVA) effort has been directed against this section of the country.

Prior to 1966, arms, munitions, and other logistic supplies for the VC operating in this area arrived by sea from North Vietnam. Sampans and junks hauled some of the supplies, but the majority of them arrived aboard 100-ton steel-hulled trawlers which unloaded directly on RVN beaches. Starting in early 1966, Operation MARKET TIME established a naval blockade of the entire coast of RVN that effectively cut off this direct sea line of communications. The VC/NVA countered by obtaining the tacit approval of the Sihanouk government to ship supplies through the port of Sihanoukville to Cambodian storage areas near the RVN/Cambodian Border. The first shipment of arms arrived at Sihanoukville in October 1966 and opened up the major LOC for supporting the war in III and IV Corps.

Hak Ly Company, a VC/NVA front, trucked supplies from the port via Highway 4 to Kampong Speu, where they were stored in two logistic depots. One of the depots was operated by the VC/NVA and the other by the Cambodian army compound at Lovek, northwest of Phnom Penh. The goods were reshipped from the depots on Hak Ly trucks over Cambodia's all-weather road network directly to base areas alongside key infiltration points on the RVN Border (Fig. 3). By 1969, these areas served not only as logistical bases but also as training areas, rest and relaxation camps, hospitals, infiltration camps, and tactical jump-off points for attacks in III and IV CTZs.

The presence of large VC/NVA forces estimated at 40,000 by Gen. Lon Nol in 1969, slowly created increasing tensions within Cambodia. Many Cambodian officials began to fear the occupation of large portions of her eastern frontier was a serious threat to the sovereignty and territorial integrity of Cambodia. These fears were exacerbated by the VC/NVA, who harassed the local inhabitants by collecting taxes, conscripting them for labor, and restricting their movements. The VC/NVA excluded Cambodian government officials from large sectors of the border and exercised de facto control of these areas. They also began to aid the local Communist insurgents, the Khmer Rouge. High prices offered by the VC/NVA led to the development of a black market in rice, a distorted domestic pricing and marketing system, and corruption in government.

These factors prompted Prince Sihanouk to limit activities of the VC/NVA. After years of denial, in March 1969, Sihanouk publicly admitted the VC/NVA were using Cambodian territory. In May 1969, his government instituted an embargo against the major transshipments of arms from Kampong Speu and Lovek to the border base areas. This embargo lasted until

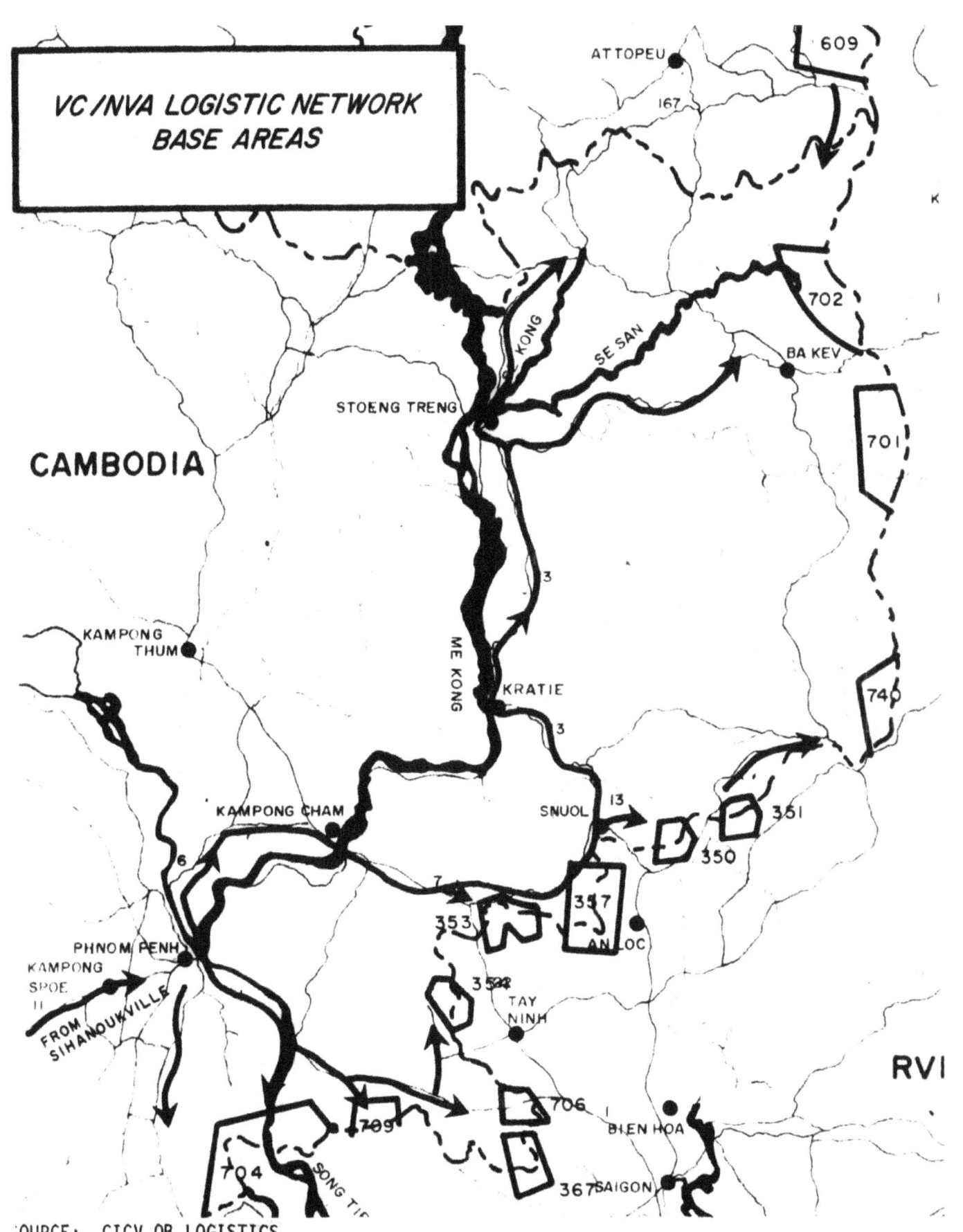

FIGURE 3

## CAMBODIAN BASE CAMPS
## ESTIMATES PRIOR TO OPERATIONS

| Base Areas | 704 | 709 | 367 706 | 354 | 352 353 | 350 | 351 | 740 | 701 | 702 | 609 |
|---|---|---|---|---|---|---|---|---|---|---|---|
| Base Camps/Training | 16 | 6 | 27 | 10 | 12 | 1 | 11 | 5 | 8 | 28 | 1 |
| Hospitals/Dispensaries | 4 | 2 | 9 | 1 | 3 |  |  | 1 |  |  |  |
| Storage Areas | 10 |  | 27 | 5 | 1 | 2 | 8 | 1 |  | 2 |  |
| POW Camp | 1 |  | 4 | 1 | 1 |  |  |  |  |  |  |
| Strongpoints | 4 | 11 | 17 | 9 | 1 | 1 |  |  | 1 | 13 | 1 |
| Other Installations | 11 | 1 | 8 | 9 | 7 | 1 | 2 | 7 |  | 4 | 11 |
| Troop Strength | 1250 | 1050 | 5830 | 1300 | 6996 | 1550 | 2200 | 250 | 1500 | 800 | 1200 |
| Bivouac Areas |  |  |  |  |  | 1 | 1 | 29 | 1 | 20 | 5 |

SOURCE: MACJ231-6-1 SUPPLEMENTAL DATA SHEET

SUBJECT: Cambodia Base Areas, 17 May 70 (C)

FIGURE 4

September when Sihanouk apparently offered to release 3,000 to 5,000 tons of supplies in return for a North Vietnamese agreement to: (1) confine their activities to specified enclaves and to move between enclaves only with permission of the Cambodian government; (2) vacate the enclaves as their need for sanctuaries declined; and (3) stop aiding the Khmer Rouge. Sihanouk then created a Special Missions Office in the Royal Army of Cambodia (FARK) to control and monitor all VC/NVA shipments. A FARK officer accompanied all convoys to make certain they arrived at the proper destination.

In August, Sihanouk had established the Salvation Government under Lon Nol as Prime Minister and Prince Sisowath Sirik Matak as Deputy Prime Minister to reform the economic system of Cambodia. As past Commander-in-Chief of the Army, Lon Nol had strong military backing. Matak was Sihanouk's cousin and was influential in both business and government bureaucratic circles. Shortly after Lon Nol took office, his wife died and he took a 30-day mourning leave. At the end of October 1969, Lon Nol went to France and did not return to Cambodia until 18 February 1970.

During Lon Nol's absences, relations between Matak and Sihanouk slowly deteriorated, primarily because of Matak's growing influence over domestic issues and his efforts to restrict the VC/NVA to their sanctuaries. While Sihanouk had granted Lon Nol and Matak a strong mandate to solve the domestic problems, he considered the VC/NVA to fall in the realm of foreign policy, which he intended to control himself. Tension also grew over the involvement of Sihanouk's fifth and then recognized wife, Monique, her mother, and half-brother in selling protection, weapons, and land rights to the VC/NVA and in smuggling gold, jewels, and drugs. These activities undermined Matak's efforts to stop smuggling and to control the VC/NVA.

Despite these growing tensions, on 6 January 1970, Sihanouk departed for Europe, ostensibly for his health. The first hints of trouble following Lon Nol's return occurred on 8 March 1970, when demonstrations against the VC/NVA presence in Cambodia broke out in several towns along the border.

On 11 March, a large crowd sacked the embassies of the Provisional Revolutionary Government of South Vietnam and North Vietnam. Following these actions, Lon Nol announced the government intended to follow a truly neutral policy. He then ordered all VC/NVA troops to be out of the country by 15 March 1970. When Sihanouk opposed these actions from Paris, France, Lon Nol and Matak arranged a deposition. On 18 March 1970, the National Assembly met in secret session and unanimously voted to replace Sihanouk as Chief of State. Sihanouk responded by broadcasting a call for arms over Radio Peking and dissolving the cabinet headed by Lon Nol on grounds of high treason. Sihanouk further aligned himself with the communists in late April by participating in the formation of the Indochinese People's United Front by representatives from Vietnam, Laos, and Cambodia. On 5 May 1970, he announced the formation of the

Royal Government of National Union and proclaimed it to be the true government of the people of Cambodia.

The VC/NVA reacted to Lon Nol's order by initiating pro-Sihanouk demonstrations, primarily in Kampong Cham Province in the towns of Snuol, Krek, Chup, and Kampong Cham. All of these towns were located near large rubber plantations staffed by North Vietnamese laborers. The demonstrations succeeded in drawing the Cambodian Army units back to protect the urban areas, thereby relieving pressure on the border sanctuaries. VC/NVA units then began moving along the border and by 12 April controlled a corridor 10 to 15 kilometers wide from the FISHHOOK to the Gulf of Siam.

Next, the VC/NVA moved to secure all major LOCs leading to their base areas. In Kampong Cham Province, they cut Highway 13 between Snuol and Kratie and by 28 April controlled Snuol, Mimot, Krek, and stretches of Highway 7 leading from the town of Kampong Cham to Krek. In Svay Rieng Province, they pushed up Highway 1, taking the towns of Chi Phu and Presaut and threatening Svay Rieng City. VC/NVA elements also took the town of Saang, approximately 20 kilometers south of Phnom Penh. Similar movement cut Highways 2 and 3 at the cities of Takeo and Ang Tasaom, southwest of Phnom Penh, and harassed Highway 4 in Kampong Speu Province. By 28 April 1970, it was apparent that the VC/NVA were attempting to isolate the capital city of Phnom Penh to apply increasing pressure on the Lon Nol government.

The movement of the VC/NVA to control the corridor to the Gulf of Siam was the first time they had openly clashed with the National Army of Cambodia (FANK). Lon Nol soon realized the national army was not prepared to stand alone against the enemy. On 13 April, he issued a worldwide appeal for military aid. The following day, he abandoned his strictly neutral posture and appealed directly to the United States for help. While no official U.S. commitment was issued, some captured and extra small arms and ammunition were sent to the FANK.

Immediately after the fall of Sihanouk, officials in Washington and at Military Assistance Command, Vietnam, began shaping plans to exploit the political situation by cleaning out the base sanctuaries of the enemy on the Cambodian Border. MACV proposed a plan to the Joint Chiefs of Staff on 29 March 1970. [1/] The President of the United States considered the proposal and as stated in his message of 30 April 1970, he saw three alternatives. First, we could do nothing. The ultimate result of such a course was clear. Second, we could provide massive military assistance to Cambodia; however, he did not see that the Cambodians could effectively use such aid against the immediate threat. The third choice was to go to the heart of the trouble and clear out the VC/NVA sanctuaries. This was the decision of President Richard M. Nixon: [2/]

> *"After full consultation with the National Security Council, Ambassador Bunker, General Abrams and my other advisers, I have concluded that the actions*

Supply cache located in Cambodia.
FIGURE 5

*of the enemy in the last ten days clearly endanger the lives of Americans who are in Vietnam now and would constitute an unacceptable risk to those who will be there after our withdrawal of 150,000.*

*"To protect our men who are in Vietnam and to guarantee the continued success of our withdrawal and Vietnamization programs, I have concluded the time has come for action."*

Authority to take action to launch the operation reached the field about 25 April 1970. In Washington, on 30 April 1970, President Nixon announced that U.S. forces had entered the FISHHOOK area of Cambodia. This operation under control of II Field Force Vietnam began in the early morning of 1 May, Vietnam time. The Cambodian government was notified of the impending action just prior to its initiation. South Vietnamese troops had moved into the Parrot's Beak on 29 April, but no U.S. troops were involved.

CHAPTER II

AIR SUPPORT OF GROUND FORCES

## Ground Operations

As early as mid-April 1970, some armed forces of the Government of Vietnam were reported to be opearating in Cambodia. Certain Vietnamese infantry cooperated directly with Cambodian infantry; in other cases, Vietnamese artillery fired across the border in support of Cambodian forces. However, the Allied Cambodian Expedition officially started on 29 April. In the next two months, 12 different operations spaced along the length of the Cambodian-Vietnamese Border undertook to drive the enemy out of the sanctuaries, destroy or capture his war materials stored there, and disrupt his retraining and reorganization facilities. Although U.S. ground forces were restricted to within 30 kilometers of the frontier, Vietnamese forces went much deeper (Fig. 2), up to 90 kilometers at the city of Kampong Speu. At the end of June, U.S. forces were withdrawn, but the Vietnamese continued one of the operations.

The first of the 12 operations was TOAN THANG 42, which was originally called ROCK CRUSHER. On 29 April, ARVN units from III and IV Corps entered the Parrot's Beak where Base Areas 367 and 706 had given the VC/NVA a secure base only 65 kilometers from Saigon. Figure 6 sketches the first week's movements. IV Corps participation ended on 6 May, but the III Corps units, after temporarily withdrawing, returned to the

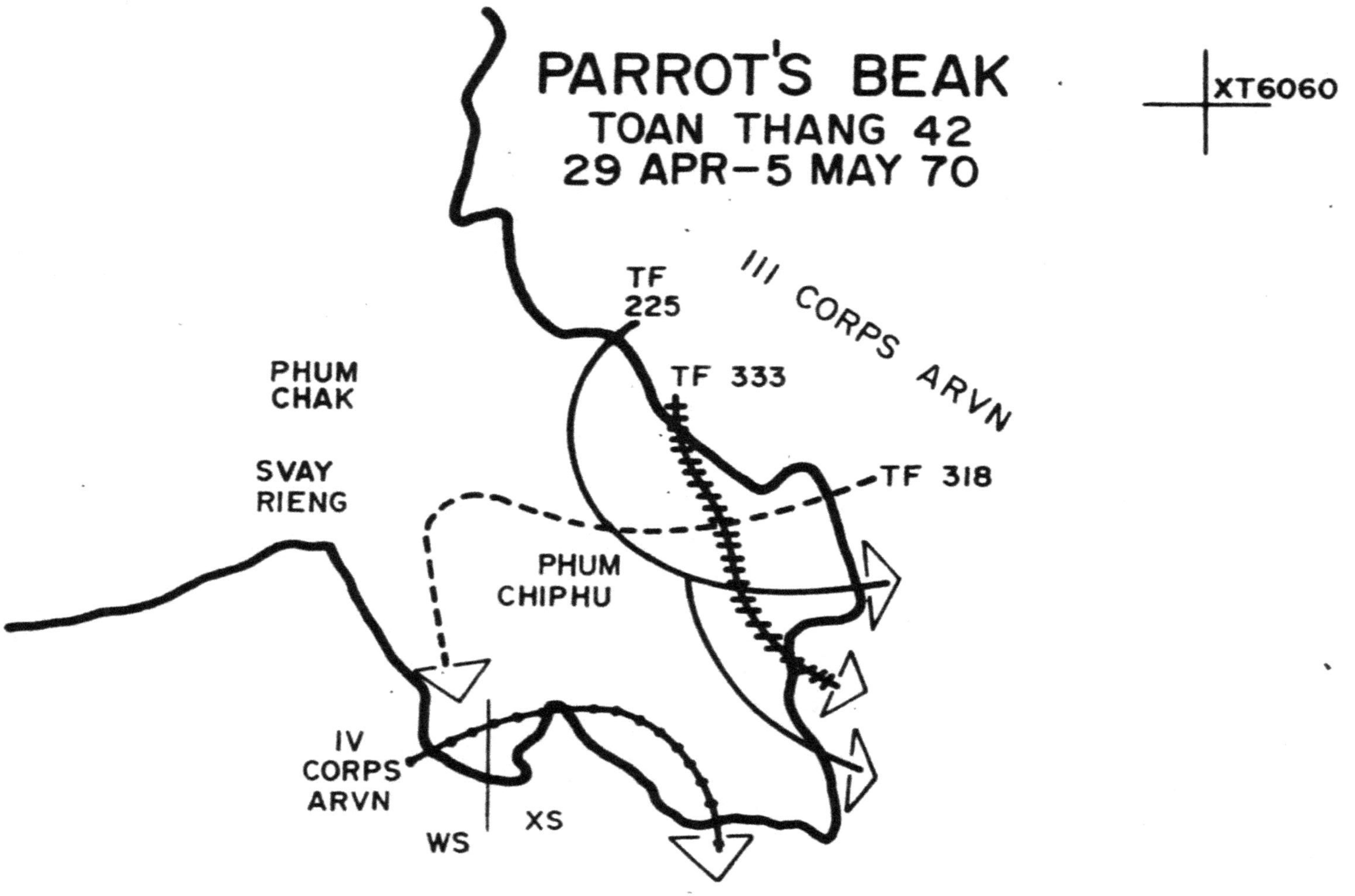

**PARROT'S BEAK**
**TOAN THANG 42**
**29 APR – 5 MAY 70**

XT6060

TF 225
TF 333
TF 318
III CORPS ARVN
PHUM CHIPHU
PHUM CHAK
SVAY RIENG
IV CORPS ARVN
XS
WS

SOURCE: COMUSMACV JOPREP
JIFFY SPECIAL REPORT 1-12

FIGURE 6

area.  Continuing to operate under the same code name, TOAN THANG 42, III Corps forces before the end of June had been as far north as 12 degrees north latitude, across the Mekong River from Kampong Cham.  TOAN THANG 42 was primarily an ARVN operation throughout, with U.S. participation holding to a level of 650-850 troops for most of the period.  Figure 1 tabulates selected operational results for all 12 operations.  As is shown, TOAN THANG 42 was one of the most significant in several categories, and it was the most costly in Allied casualties.

The next operation, TOAN THANG 43, was aimed at the second sharp Cambodian protuberance into Vietnam, the FISHHOOK, which housed Base Areas 352 and 353.  Elements of the 3d ARVN Abn Bde entered by air assault while elements of the 1st U.S. Cav Div marched overland on 1 May; the enemy was apparently caught flat-footed.  Although Allied forces worked their way north of Snuol and west into the Dog's Head, this operation was much more localized than TOAN THANG 42.  For the full two months, Allied units scoured the FIGHHOOK and achieved the most significant results of all 12 operations.  For most of the period, troop strength averaged about 3,700 ARVN and 12,500 US.

The northernmost operation was BINH TAY I.  Following B-52 strikes, elements of the 4th U.S. Infantry Division and 40th Army of Republic of Vietnam (ARVN) Regiment were air assaulted into Base Area 702.  The ARVN units met light resistance, but the first U.S. elements found hot landing zones and were diverted, while subsequent assaults were delayed for additional preparation by airstrikes. All units had been inserted by D+2, and thereafter ground contacts were light and scattered. On the fifth day, the largest single rice cache of the entire campaign was found--over 500 tons. A large hospital, complete with a laboratory containing X-ray equipment, showed the area to be a major medical rehabilitation center. The number of training sites, base camps, and food production areas further testified to the logistical importance of Base Area 702.

On 6-7 May, four operations began--TOAN THANG 44, 45, 46, 500; of these TOAN THANG 45 was the most significant. Elements of the 1st U.S. Air Cavalry Division were air assaulted into Base Area 351 without opposition. On the second day, a cache estimated at 267 tons was uncovered. The area of operations reached west to 106° 30'E and included about 20 kilometers on both sides of the border. From an initial strength of 2,400 troops, the total rose to above 10,000 for the first three weeks of June.

CUU LONG I was launched on 9 May. Troops ranged to the west bank of the Mekong River, north almost to 12N. A principal objective was seizure of the ferry site northwest of Prey Veng, which was accomplished the first day. Thereafter two sunken ferry boats were located, raised, and repairs begun. Under cover of the operation, Vietnamese flotillas evacuated more than 35,000 refugees from as far north as Kampong Cham. The USN provided most of the U.S. strength in this operation. At the

Troops investigate ammunition stockpile.
FIGURE 7

end of June, when U.S. participation ended, the Vietnamese merged the operation into their CUU LONG III.

From mid-May, Vietnamese units operated between the Mekong River and the seaport of Kampot, as far inland as Kampong Speu. Originally called CUU LONG II, the operation was renamed CUU LONG III after the first week. U.S. participation was never large and dropped steadily. At the end of June, Vietnamese operations were continuing from the Parrot's Beak to the sea under the name CUU LONG III.

Much of the military equipment captured by U.S. and GVN forces in Cambodia was transferred to the Cambodian forces. By 1 July, 11,688 individual weapons with 2.6 million rounds of ammunition, and 1,292 crew-served weapons with 2.1 million rounds, had been turned over. 1/

## Air Support

On 27 March 1970, an ad hoc planning group meeting was held at MACV headquarters. During this meeting, 7AF representatives emphasized the need for complete photo reconnaissance and urged that ARVN airborne units and interdiction airstrikes be used to seal the backside of the FISHHOOK. Neither idea was incorporated into the campaign plan which the ad hoc group proposed and the Commander, U.S. Military Assistance Command (COMUSMACV) forwarded to the JCS on 29 March. 2/

The 7AF did not receive instructions to begin definitive planning until 27 April 1970, two days before ARVN's entry into the Parrot's Beak. Even then, the strict "eyes only" top secret security measures restricted briefings to "key officers." Every effort was made to prevent any leaks to the press and to time U.S. entry into the FISHHOOK to coincide with the President's message on Cambodia. The basic concept for air support was to provide all sorties required on a first priority basis. A JCS message of 25 April had revised the priorities for tactical air to be: (1) Cambodia; (2) South Vietnam; (3) BARREL ROLL; and (4) STEEL TIGER.[3/]

As it had done in the past, the flexibility and responsiveness of tactical air was demonstrated. The Tactical Air Control System met the requirements of the Cambodian operations with routine efficiency. Only a few special arrangements were needed. On the evening of 28 April, TACC alerted the Direct Air Support Centers (DASC) and fighter wings to be ready to support ARVN operations in the Parrot's Beak if ordered to do so. The FAC and fighter pilots were to follow normal in-country Rules of Engagement and operating procedures and were cautioned to exercise extreme vigilance to avoid dropping ordnance on the noncombatant populace. Air Liaison Officers (ALO) were to encourage the ARVN units to which they were assigned to use Vietnam Air Force (VNAF) assets. The Parrot's Beak operation was to be a Vietnamese show with U.S. involvement kept to a minimum. Backup search and rescue (SAR) forces were augmented by moving four A-1 aircraft from Nakhon Phanom and two HH-3E helicopters from Da Nang to Bien Hoa and placing one AC-130 gunship on ground alert at Tuy Hoa.[4/]

The FISHHOOK operation required a few additional preparations, as

12

it was primarily a U.S. action. Besides the SAR aircraft already on station, TACC allocated two Blindbat flareships at Cam Ranh Bay, four AC-119K gunships at Phan Rang, and ten additional alert sorties at Bien Hoa and Phan Rang. They also organized Spat and Sleepytime FACs for night strikes and set up a refueling track southwest of Ban Me Thout. A message of 30 April to the Direct Air Support Centers (DASCs) and fighter wings informed them that U.S./ARVN forces would begin operating in certain areas of Cambodia adjacent to III Corps and repeated the instructions to use normal operating procedures and to exercise extreme vigilance to avoid dropping ordnance on the noncombatant populace. For security purposes they were to submit only one copy of their After Action Reports, OpRep-4, by 7AF courier. Fighters on Cambodian missions were sent to in-country rendezvous near the FISHHOOK. The pilots were not briefed until just prior to the initial missions that they were going into Cambodia. [5/]

FACs used the built-in mobility of the Tactical Air Control System to support the ground units to which they were normally assigned by operating from their radio jeeps and flying, when necessary, out of the forward operating bases. The FISHHOOK action (TOAN THANG 42) came under control of Task Force Shoemaker which was set up by the Commanding General of the 1st Air Cavalry Division. The ALO of the 1st Air Cav Div appointed his deputy as the Task Force ALO. [6/]

To facilitate coordination of airstrikes and artillery fire within the narrow confines of the areas of operation (AO) designated for the first day's operation, the Task Force ALO set up a special Tactical Air Control Party (TACP) in the Tactical Operations Center (TOC) at Quan Loi, Task Force Headquarters. Under call sign Rash Advon, this TACP took over control of the operation from Rash Control, the normal TACP located at Phouc Vinh. The ALO of the 3d ARVN Airborne Battalion (Abn Bn) also moved his Red Marker TACP and aircraft to Quan Loi. The Rash 30 TACP supporting the 3d Brigade (Bde), and the Nile TACP supporting the 11th U.S. Armored Cavalry Regiment (ACR) were already located at Quan Loi. Nile FACs flew their O-2 aircraft out of Bien Hoa as usual, because the runway at Quan Loi was too rough for the O-2.7/

To enhance control and reduce air traffic complications, an O-2 aircraft was set up out of Di An to act as an airborne controller with the call sign Head Beagle. FAC Instructor Pilot controllers flew in the right seat. This arrangement greatly facilitated handling of the numerous airstrikes delivered during the first four days of the operation. Head Beagle circled at about 8,000 feet altitude inside the RVN Border south of the FISHHOOK. Rash Advon passed the fighters to Head Beagle, who in turn directed them to the proper FAC from the standard rendezvous established for each AO. By contacting the FAC about 15 minutes before the scheduled time over target (TOT) of each mission, Head Beagle was able to monitor the weather and the FAC's ability to handle the strike as scheduled. If a FAC were running behind, or if one needed an immediate airstrike or a particular type of ordnance,

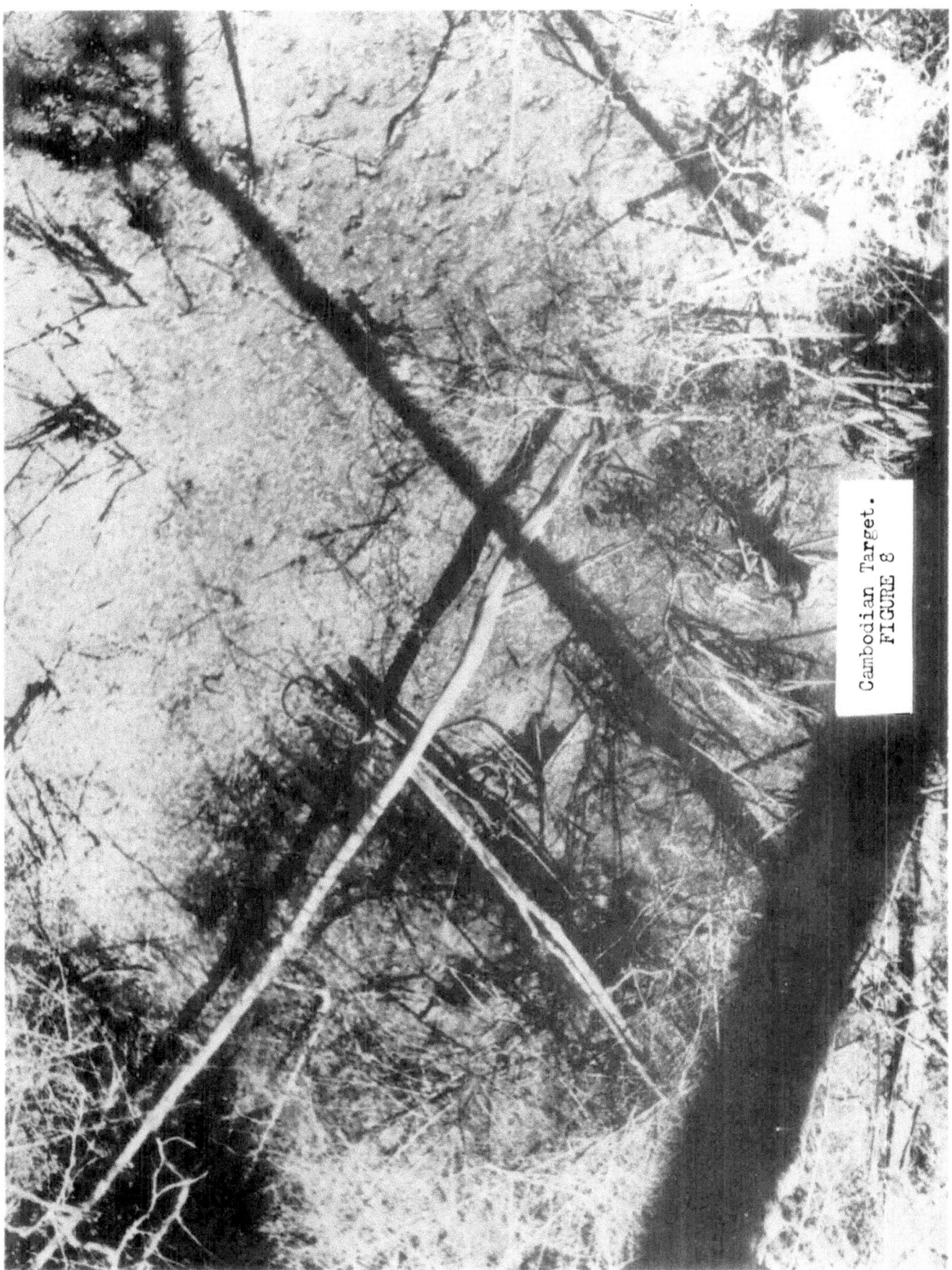

Cambodian Target.
FIGURE 8

Head Beagle would hold the fighters at the rendezvous or divert them as needed.[8/] This tactic had been combat tested at the siege of Khe Sanh and other localized operations.

The lack of current intelligence during the first few days of all the operations made targeting difficult. Although there were numerous sources, the vast majority of those made available were outdated, most of them by weeks and even five and six months. While the evidence was sufficient to indicate general locations of the base areas, it did not adequately identify the exact locations of the enemy's defensive positions. This problem was complicated by delays at MACV in the dissemination of Air Force photo reconnaissance to the field commanders. This problem continued throughout the first week of the operation, with pictures arriving 24 hours after ground units moved into a new area.[9/]

Because intelligence estimated that the FISHHOOK was occupied by an enemy force of about 7,000, the concept was to suppress enemy resistance by use of massive airstrikes for landing zone (LZ) and objective preparations. The 1st Air Cav Div G-2 had compiled a list of 381 targets from an all-source intelligence readout provided by the Combined Intelligence Center, Vietnam. An air operations FAC and an artillery officer plotted all 381 targets and labeled them by type on a map. They then identified areas of concentration and established the following priorities for strikes: (1) antiaircraft and automatic weapons positions; (2) strongpoints; (3) headquarters; (4) base camps; (5) bunker complexes; and (6) storage areas. The main objective was to hit points of suspected resistance in the objective areas of each unit.

The next requirement after softening up the objectives was to have continuous air cover available for close air support of troops in contact and targets of opportunity. The FAC proposed a schedule which divided 37 airstrikes of two sorties each from 0700-1900H at fifteen-minute to one-half hour intervals between the three AOs. To be absolutely certain sufficient air coverage was available to cover any contingency, the number of airstrikes was changed from two to four sorties per airstrike for the first day's operation. In addition to these 148 tactical air sorties, six B-52 ARC LIGHT strikes of six sorties each were requested for six target boxes along the southern border of the FISHHOOK from 0415-0540H on 1 May 1970 (Fig.9). These airstrikes were also targeted from the dated intelligence in the CICV target list. There was no current intelligence from infrared (IR), sniffer, side-looking airborne radar (SLAR), sensors, or long-range reconnaissance patrols (LRRP).[10/] Both tactical air and B-52 requests were processed through normal channels and were approved as submitted.

ARC LIGHT strikes early on the morning of 1 May 1970 signaled the entry into Cambodia by U.S. ground forces. The first tactical

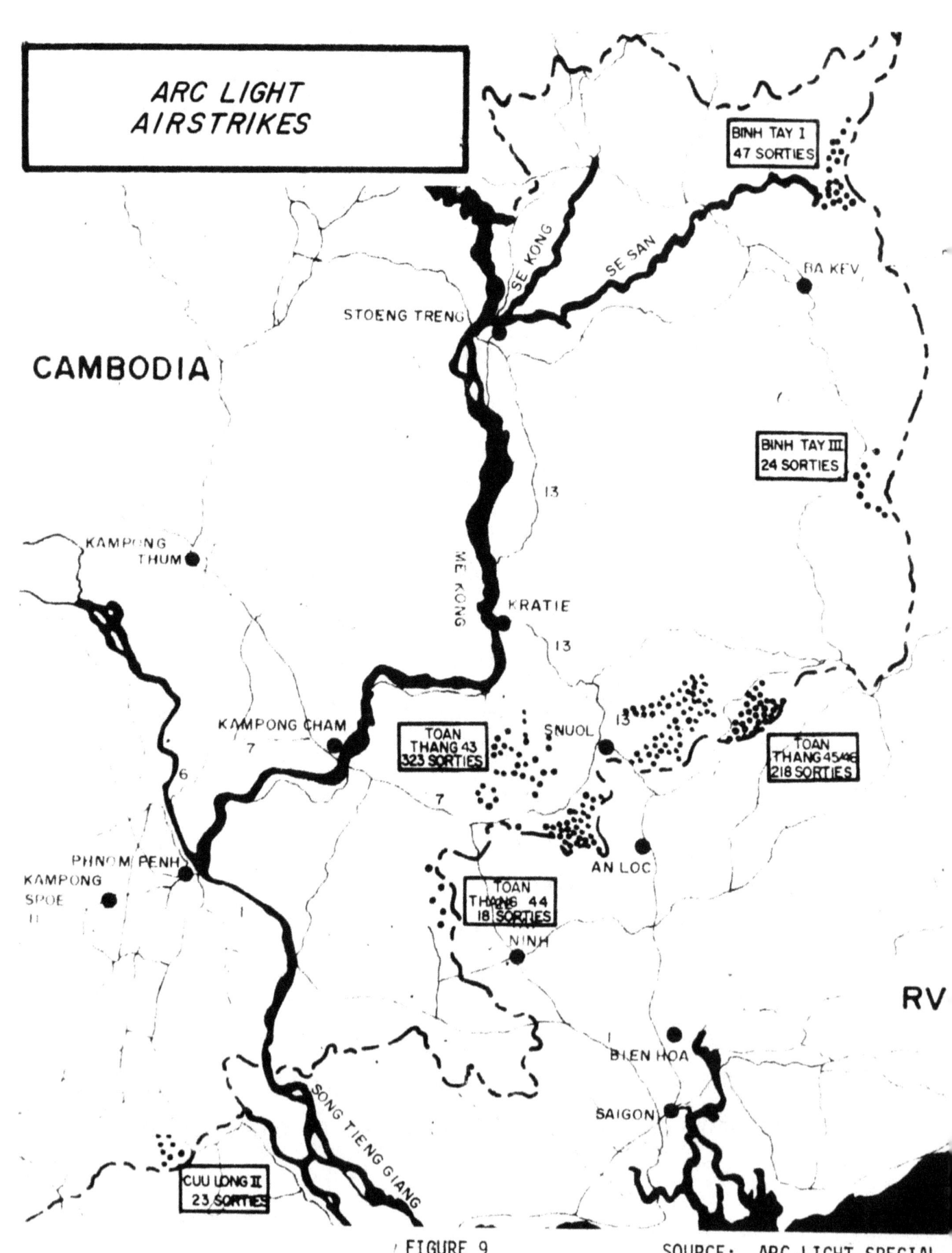

FIGURE 9

SOURCE: ARC LIGHT SPECIAL HOAB, 1 July 70, MACV IDHS

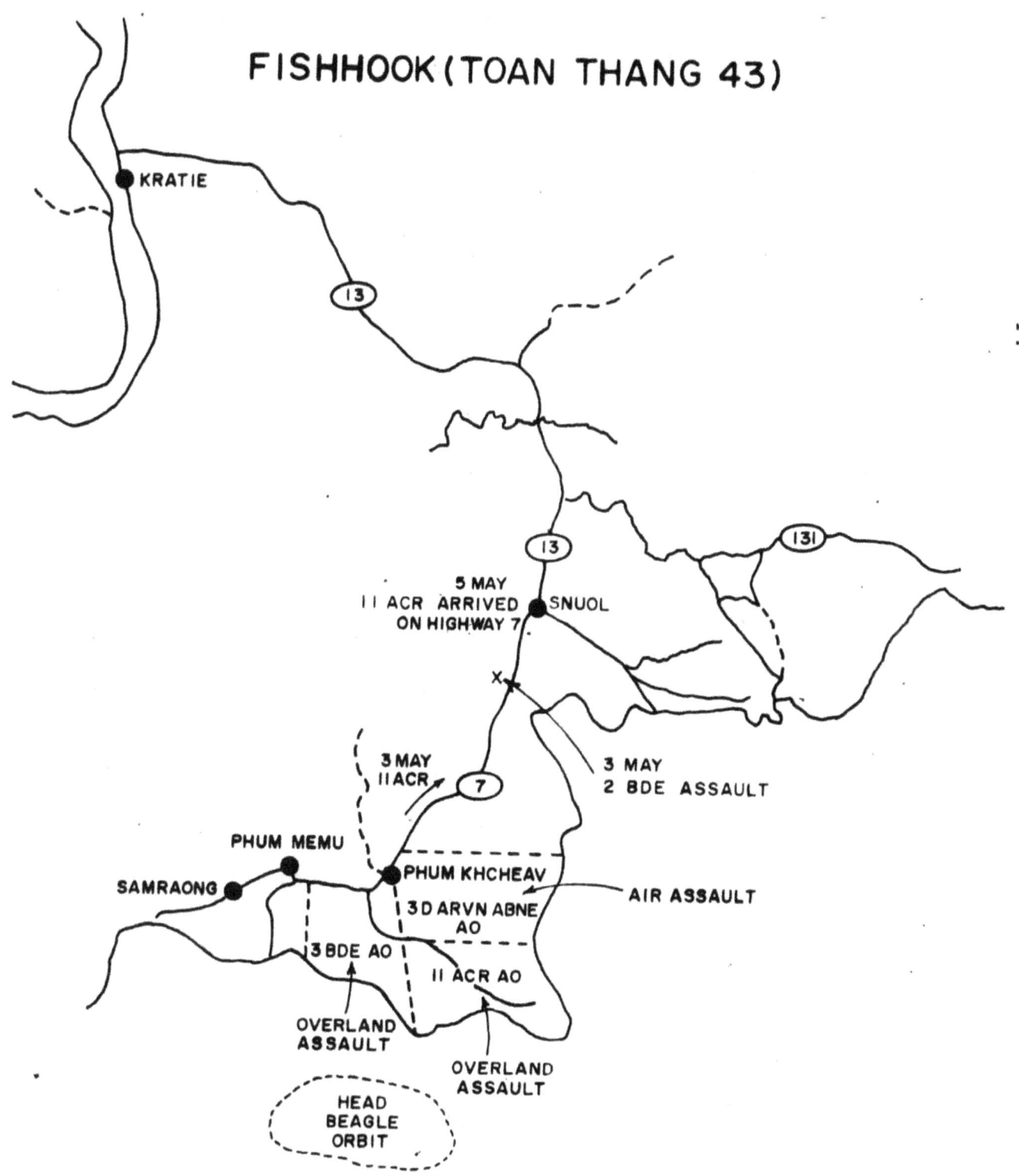

FIGURE 10

airstrikes hit their targets about 0700H and units of the Task Force moved by ground and air across the border on schedule. The 11th ACR moved overland from the south, the 3d Bde closed from the west, and the 3d ARVN Abn air assaulted from the northeast (Fig. 10). Army hunter-killer teams composed of light observation helicopters (LOH) and Cobra gunships ranged over the northwest front to cut off the enemy's escape.

Head Beagle passed the fighters off to the FACs in their respective AOs and proved to be the integral link in the successful handling of 144 preplanned and 48 immediate airstrikes delivered throughout the day. This was no mean task as the fluid nature of the ground battle continually demanded changes in the schedule. Although ground contact was limited to small engagements, demands for support of troops in contact and strikes against targets of opportunity necessitated diverting most of the airstrikes from the preplanned coordinates. The uncertainty of friendly locations and the absolute necessity to avoid noncombatant casualties delayed clearances and required some fighters to hold 15 to 30 minutes.

At his evening staff meeting on 1 May, the Commanding General of II Field Force Vietnam (FFV) stated the day's operation far exceeded his expectations, everything had gone like clockwork with the airborne assault achieving complete surprise. Not one friendly soldier was killed and only 12 were wounded, as compared to about 390 of the enemy killed in action (KIA). Allied airpower contributed greatly to these results.[11/]

The planning of preplanned targets continued to suffer from the lack of real time intelligence. Consequently, the second and third day targets were merely selected from the dated list of 381 targets passed down from division headquarters for the first day's planning. However, this was not of critical importance as the ground commanders' primary interest was to have airstrikes available throughout the day to support troops in contact (TIC) situations and to hit targets of opportunity. The divert rate from the preplanned coordinates bore this out. While the concept of operation did not change, the quality of intelligence did improve after the fourth day. Information from IR, SLAR, army photo reconnaissance, visual reconnaissance (VR), and prisoner of war (PW) reports started to accumulate. The Division G-2 used this intelligence to compile a new list of 160 targets on the fourth day and another list of 264 targets on the sixth day.[12/]

Although the number of preplanned airstrikes remained about the same for the second day, the number of sorties was cut in half by reducing the request from four to two sorties per airstrike. When the number of sorties requested increased to 89 the third day and jumped to 128 the fourth day, the TACC recommended that as enemy resistance was light, air could be more effectively managed by cutting down the number of preplanned requests and relying on immediate airstrikes from ground alert to fill in the gaps. This suggestion was

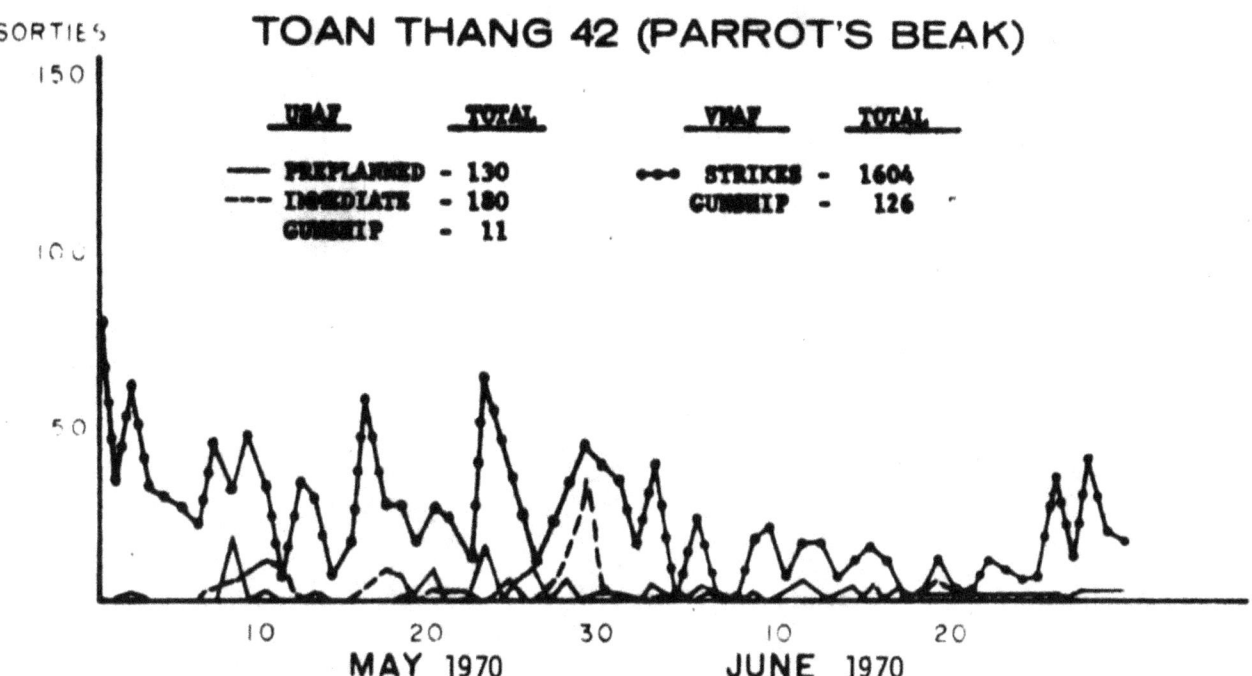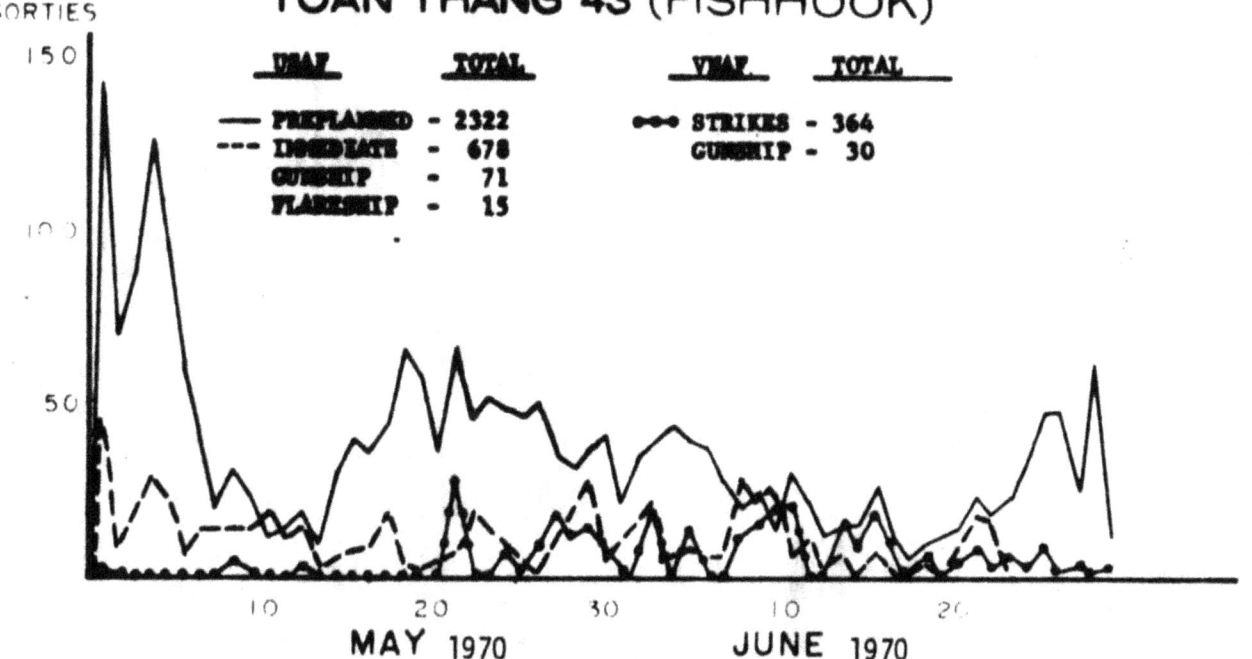

FIGURE 11

Munitions concealed in heavy undergrowth.
FIGURE 12

accepted and preplanned sorties dropped successively to a low of 20 on the eighth day and fluctuated about a lower level throughout the rest of the campaign (Fig. 11).[13/]

The concept of the operation changed drastically late in the evening of the second day, 2 May 1970. At midnight, the Task Force Commander, told his commanders that SLAR and other reports indicated the enemy was escaping the area by Highway 7 to the north. He outlined a plan for the 2d Bde to air assault into position just south of Snuol to block Highway 7 and for the 11th ACR and the 3d Bde to attack to the north (Fig. 9). This required an all night preparation and was accomplished without the benefit of photo reconnaissance of the area. The TACC suggested to the Task Force Commander that the Air Force select an interdiction point (IDP) to the north of Snuol and seal off the road. Uncertainty as to whether the Rules of Engagement would allow airstrikes in that area postponed further consideration of this idea until the fourth day.[14/]

The new plan more than tripled the size of the Task Force's AO, greatly relieving the air congestion but also vastly increasing the task of locating the enemy. The 2d Bde air assaulted south of Snuol on schedule during the morning of 3 May and the 11th ACR started a move north which brought their units up Highway 7 to the outskirts of Snuol by the afternoon of 5 May. The fast-changing ground situation negated efforts to preplan air targets and most of the airstrikes went against targets of opportunity and in support of TICs developing out of the tactical situation.

The close cooperation between the FACs and LOH scouts made them an effective combination. The 3d Bde had developed a system whereby a FAC would fly cover for a White Team (two LOH scouts). The FAC gave directions to the scouts while one scout went down low looking for targets and the other flew larger circles above him. When they found a worthwhile target or received ground fire, the FAC would get the fighters on station. The scout then marked the target with a smoke grenade and the FAC used this mark as a reference to put in his marking smoke rocket for the fighters. If time permitted, the scout checked the target and remarked between fighter passes. After the strike, the scouts descended below treetop level to make an accurate assessment of the damage.

An example of the results of such cooperation occurred on 3 May. Rash 32 was working with a White Team led by Accent 81. They were flying up Highway 7 when Accent 81 spotted tire tracks which led to some poncho covered shelters and a 2 1/2-ton truck camouflaged under the trees. Rash 32 diverted in two strikes but both of them missed the truck. Rash 32 had to respond to a TIC, and Accent 81 returned to Quan Loi for fuel. After lunch they returned to the area and Rash 32 put a strike of high drag bombs on the target. Again the truck was missed, but the blast cleared away the foliage so the scouts could clearly see stacks of crates full of weapons. About

1600H, Accent 81 landed and found a cache containing about 100 cases of new SKS and AK-47 rifles (20 each), a large wheel-mounted recoilless rifle, three 50-cal weapons, a pile of about 500 old AK-47 rifles, and uncounted other weapons under tarps. Rash 32 requested two immediate airstrikes. The first strike of CBU munitions resulted in four secondary explosions. Later ground exploitation of the area uncovered one of the largest weapons caches discovered during the operation. [15]

Requests for BULLPUP and PAVE WAY bombs for strikes on point targets, such as bridges, could not be honored by the TACC, because the delivery aircraft were based in Thailand, and the Rules of Engagement would not allow use of Thai-based aircraft in Cambodia. [16]

By the end of the fifth day, the boundaries of the operation in the FISHHOOK had been fairly well established and the ground troops settled down to searching out the area. Operations returned to the normal status of everyday procedures. The Task Force headquarters at Quan Loi was disbanded, and the Commanding General of the 1st Air Cav Div resumed direct control of the operation. Rash Advon ceased operation, returning overall control to Rash Control at Phuoc Vinh. The 3d Bde and 11th ACR FACs continued to operate out of Quan Loi, their normal location, and the 3d ARVN Abn Bde Red Marker FACs moved to Tay Ninh, their normal forward operating location. Head Beagle flew its last missions on the sixth day and the FACs returned to their regular duties.

Considering the small airspace, the fluid ground situation, and the vast numbers of aircraft involved in the first few day's activities, command and control worked smoothly and effectively. One serious accident occurred, however, and several Short Rounds were avoided only by the quick reaction of the FACs. On 2 May, an O-2 carrying two pilots collided in mid-air with a Cobra gunship. The pilots of the gunship were killed in the crash. Evidently the blade of the gunship cut the O-2 in half for the FACs both exited the aircraft and descended in their chutes. However, both pilots' legs were amputated below the knees. One was dead when he was picked up and the other died on the way to Tay Ninh in the rescue ship.[17/]

On 2 May, Rash 32 prevented friendly casulties by flying his OV-10 directly in front of a Cobra gunship team which had expended rockets on a friendly position and was coming around for a second pass. On the same day, another FAC saw troops moving through the forest when he rolled in to mark a target. Upon checking further, the ground adviser discovered that a friendly unit had moved into the area without his knowledge. The next day a FAC cleared to strike a village also discovered that friendly troops had moved into the area unperceived by the ground commander requesting the airstrike.[18/]

The ground commanders gave high praise to the alert, professional manner in which FACs managed the air support rendered during these first hectic days. They spoke enthusiastically about the responsiveness of the air support and expressed the firm conviction that it had thrown the enemy off balance, forced him to scatter, and had been the major factor in keeping the number of friendly casualties low.[19]

Except for slight modifications, the application of airpower in the FISHHOOK was typical of all operations in Cambodia. In an attempt to surprise a suspected COSVN headquarters, the 25th Inf Div deviated from the use of airstrikes for LZ preparations by targeting preplanned airstrikes adjacent to the suspected location to divert attention from the objective area. The only preparation used was heavy artillery immediately prior to the assault.[20]

Except for this attempt to surprise the enemy, the usual procedure was to use extensive airstrikes for LZ and objective preparations to suppress enemy resistance prior to combat assaults. Preplanned airstrikes served primarily as air cover for TIC and strikes against targets of opportunity, and most of them were diverted from the preplanned targets for these uses. After the first few days, the number of airstrike sorties tapered off and fluctuated at a lower level for the remainder of the campaign (Figs. 11-17). After the initial assaults and expansion of the AO boundaries, the ground forces settled down to searching out the areas and evacuating the caches discovered. During this phase, preplanned airstrikes served primarily as air cover and secondarily as a means of reconnaissance by bombing to aid in the discovery and destruction of storage areas. FAC visual reconnaissance missions and FAC coordination with LOH scouts proved particularly effective during this phase.

The foregoing descriptions also apply to the ARVN operations. They were supported primarily by VNAF FACs and VNAF fighter aircraft, and ground commanders adhered closely to methods in which they were trained. The main difference was due to weaknesses in the visual reconnaissance program of VNAF FACs. They generally put in preplanned strikes and then returned to their base. Consequently, VNAF FACs were not as responsive to immediate requests for airstrikes for TIC and targets of opportunity as their USAF counterparts.

During the ARVN operations, the USAF ALOs worked closely with the ground commanders and VNAF ALOs. While the VNAF Facs were engaged in directing the preplanned airstrikes, the USAF FACs picked up the visual reconnaissance role and responded to requests for immediate airstrikes. The level of enemy resistance in the Parrot's Beak was considerably higher than in the FISHHOOK and airstrikes in response to significant enemy contacts were more frequent. Enemy units of battalion size and larger put up intense ground fire against aircraft. On 29 May, while elements of Task Force 225 were in contact in the Parrot's Beak with an enemy force estimated at two battalions, one F-100, one helicopter, and one A-1 were shot down in the same battle. As one USAF FAC conducted the resulting SAR efforts, another directed immediate airstrikes in support of the engagement. After the battle was over, the ground commander estimated more than 100 KBA and at least that many

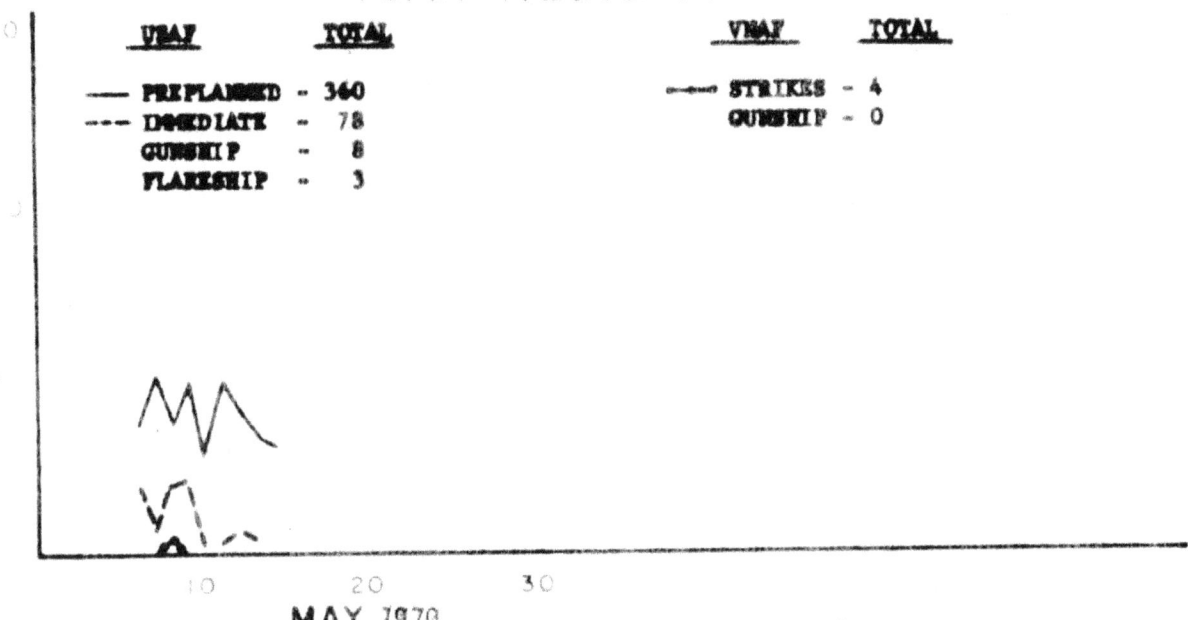

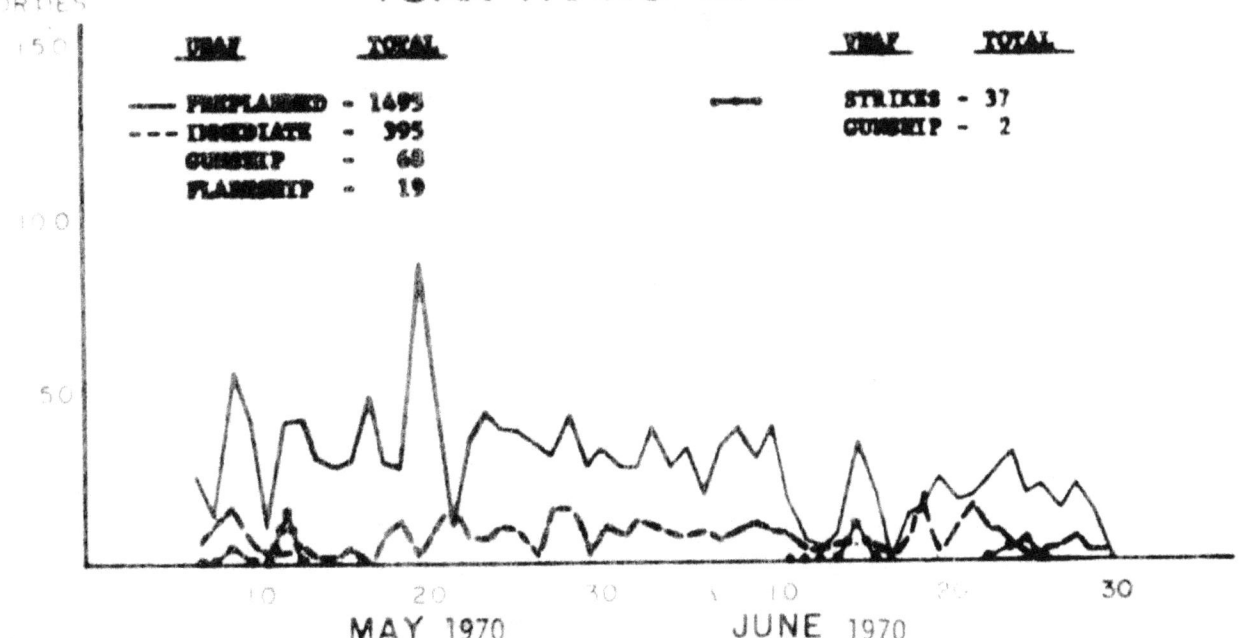

SOURCE: TACC Briefing Notes

FIGURE 13

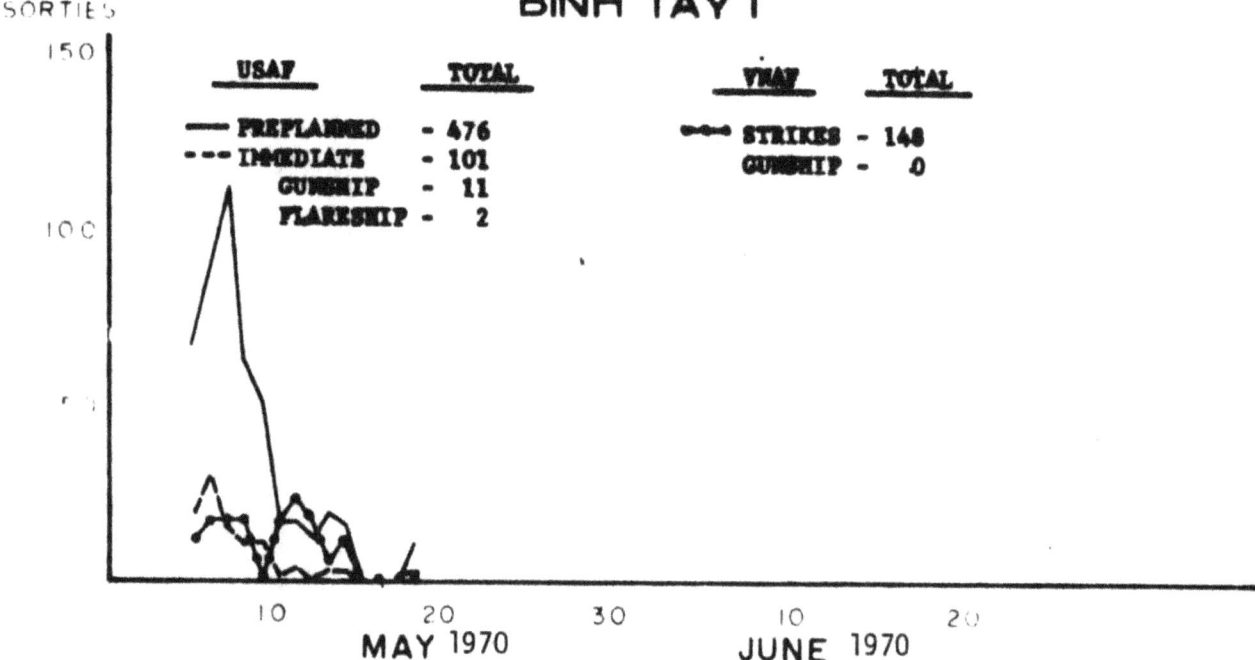
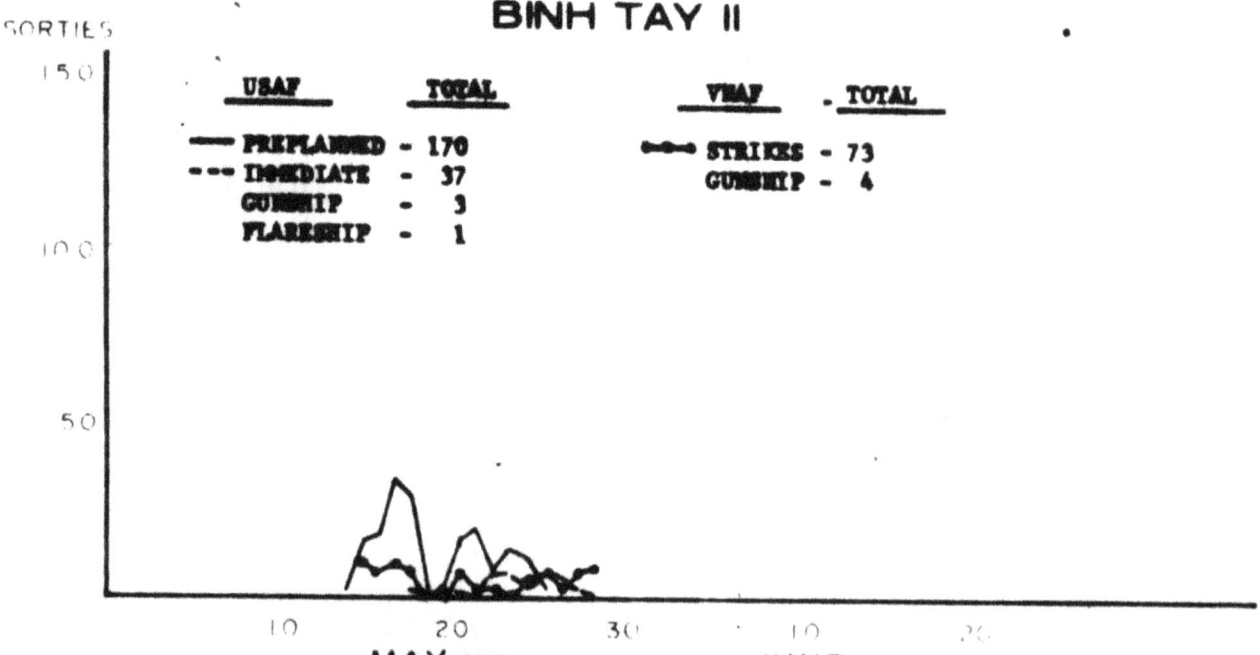

FIGURE 14

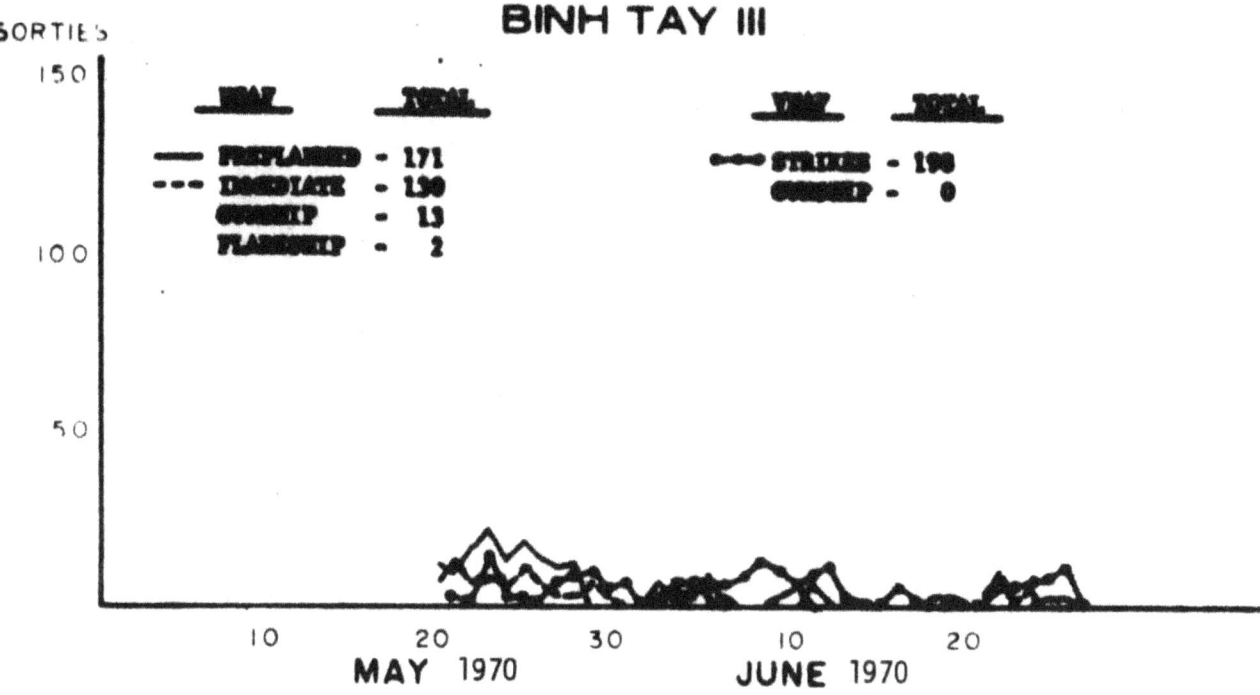

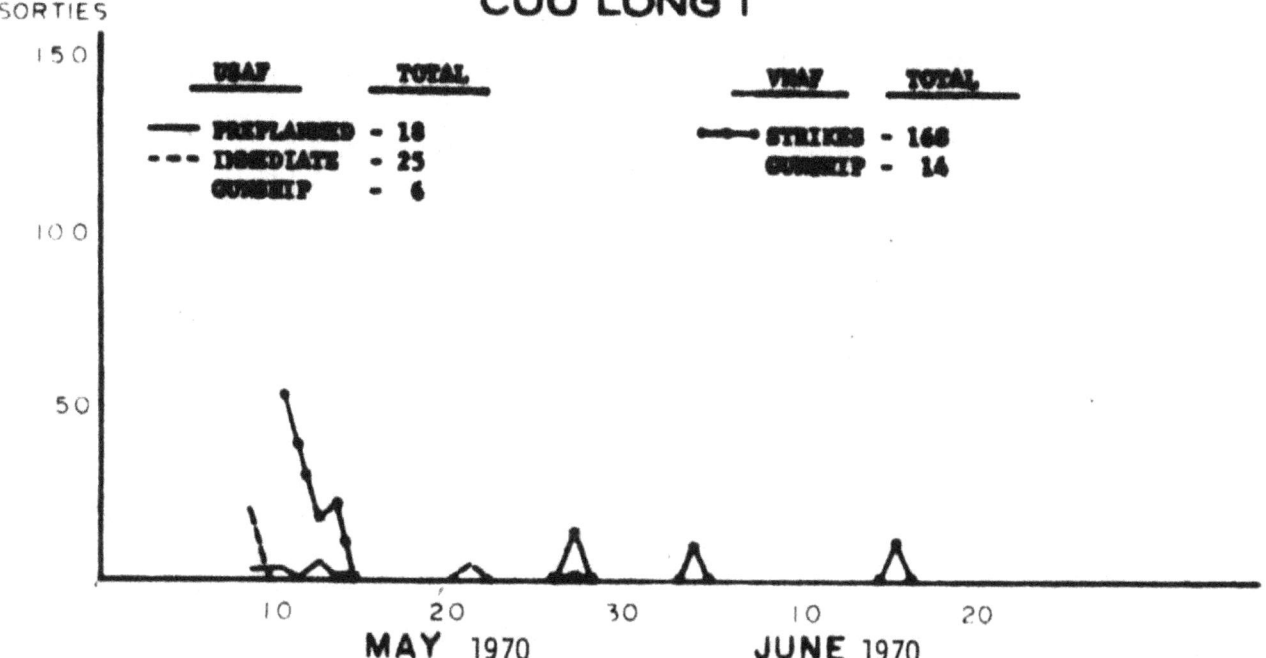

FIGURE 15

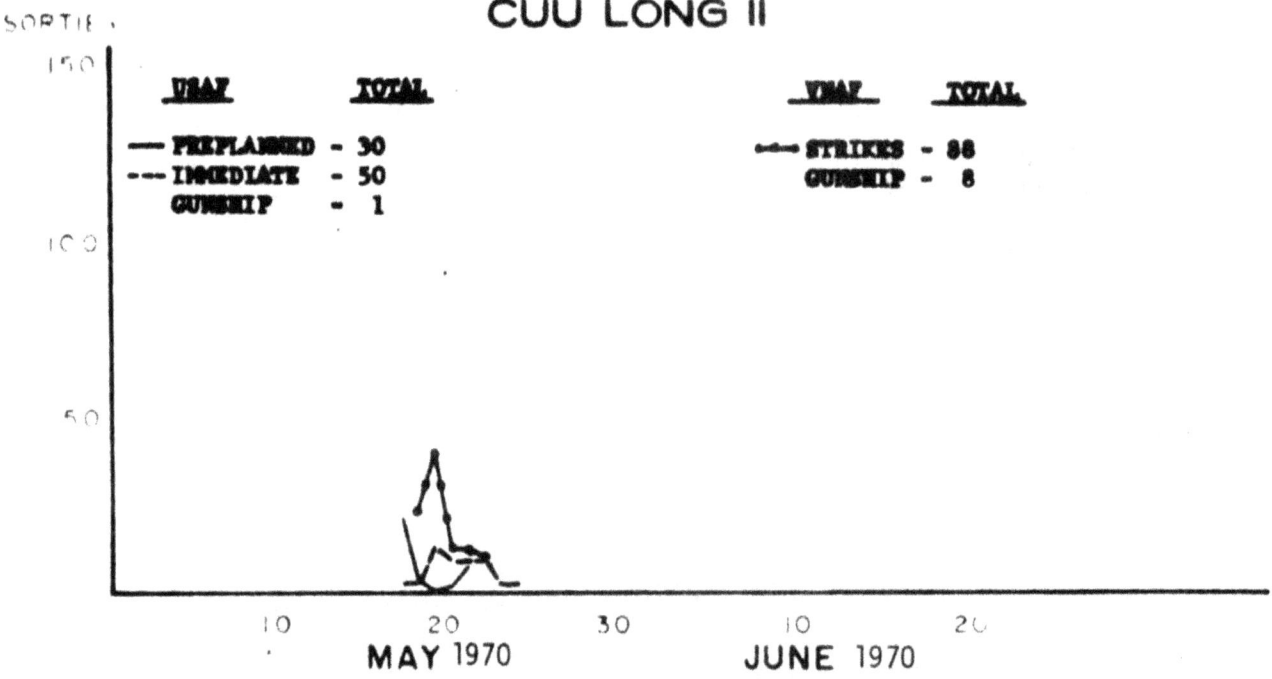

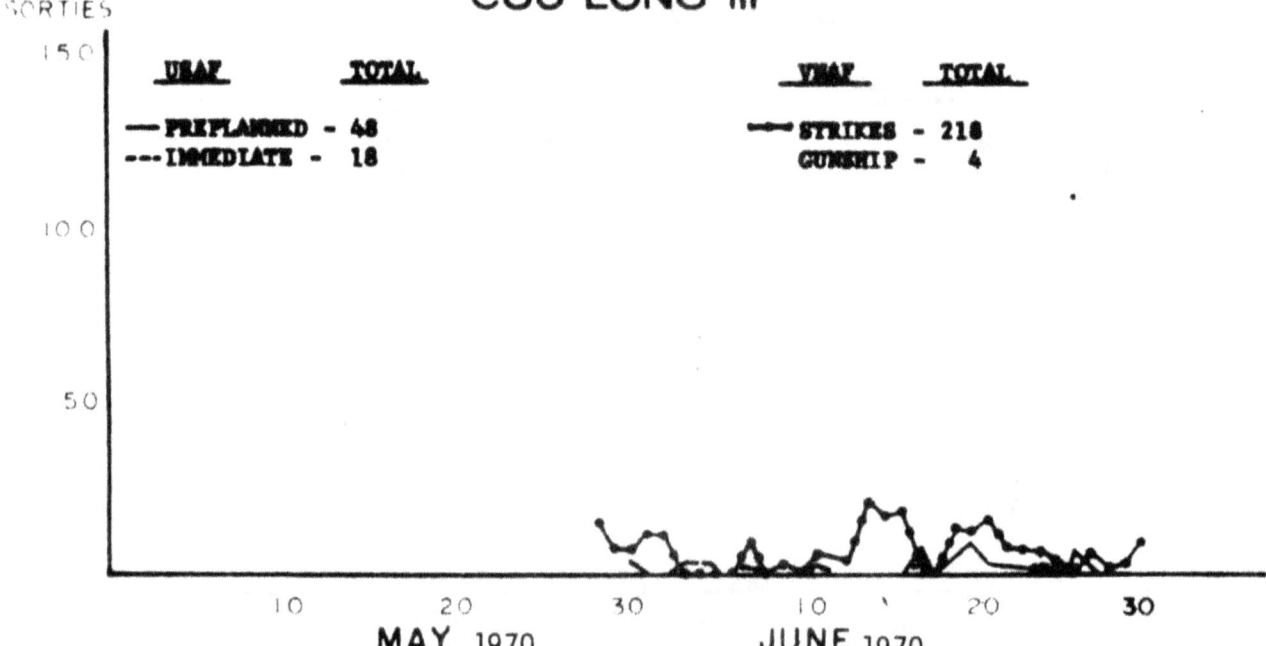

FIGURE 16

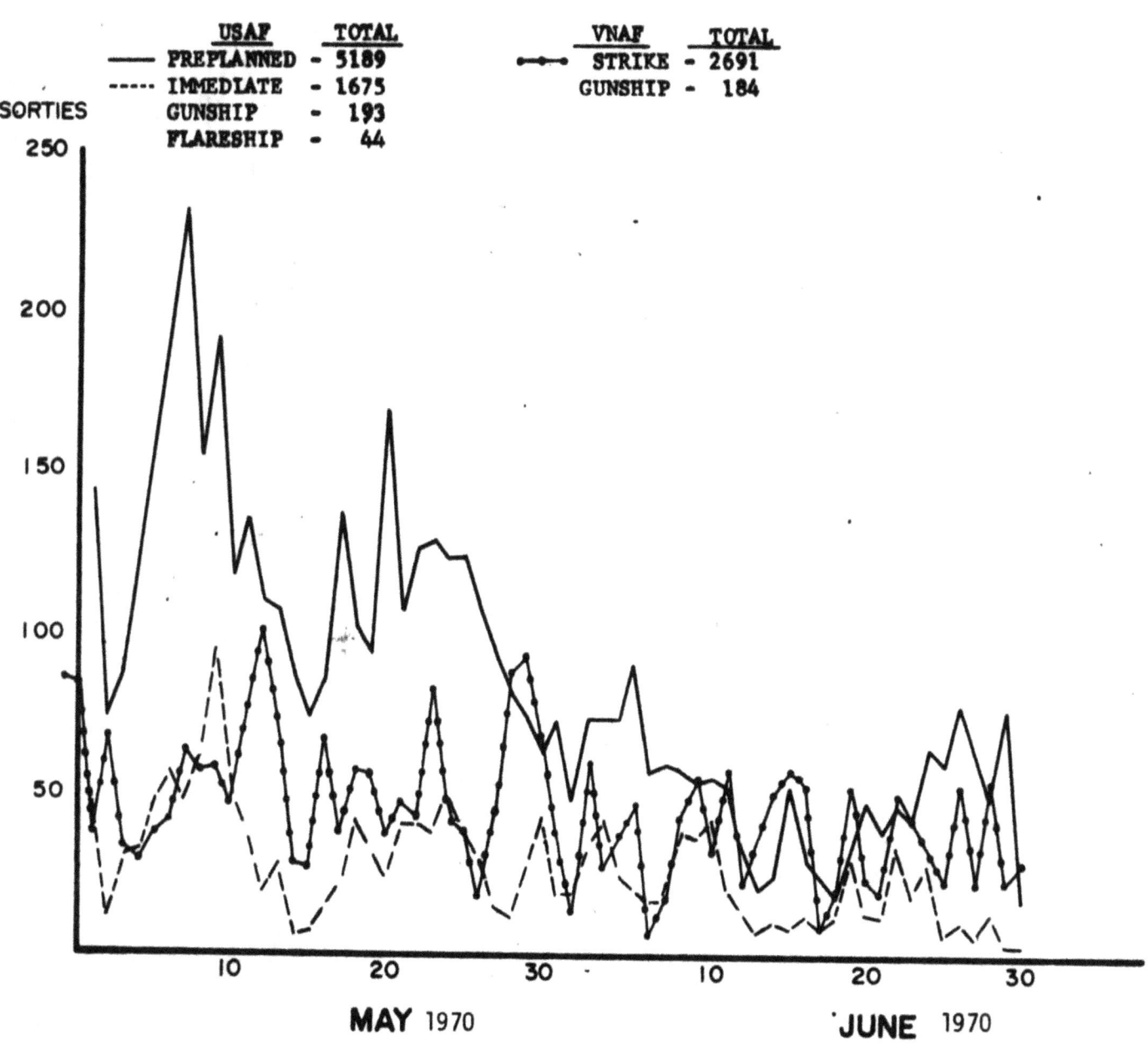

FIGURE 17

wounded.

The USAF FACs attached to the ARVN units also served in numerous other roles.  They were the first to note civilian and refugee locations and passed this information to advisers in the field and political advisers in the province to prevent inadvertent bombing of civilian noncombatants.  USAF FACs scouted the areas ahead of ground movements and advised commanders of terrain conditions and the possible location of enemy defenses.  On one occasion, a USAF FAC led an ARVN medevac helicopter through intense ground fire in one-half mile visibility to locate a friendly position.  He adjusted artillery on the enemy positions while the medevac evacuated the wounded.[21]

Ground commanders' appreciation for the air support they received was reflected in a letter to Gen. George S. Brown, Deputy Commander for Air Operations, MACV, from Lt. Gen. Michael S. Davison, Commander, II Field Force Vietnam:[22]

> *"Fran Roberts has just provided me with a succinct recapitulation of the close air support we have received in the border areas of III CTZ during the period 1 May - 10 June 1970.  I find the total effort expended on our behalf to be extremely impressive, and am enclosing the report as rendered to me, on the chance that perhaps this information hasn't reached you in quite this form.*
>
> *"I'm most appreciative, not only of the amount of support your units have provided to the II FFV and III Corps maneuver elements, but also of the extremely adept and timely manner in which it's been delivered.  It has been a professional performance of the highest quality."*

## Air Resources

Prior to beginning the Cambodian operation, 7AF advised MACV that in-country resources could provide adequate support without augmentation provided sortie and munitions limitations were temporarily lifted. This estimate proved to be substantially correct as the only augmentation required in support of the ground operations through 30 June 1970 was three C-130 flareships from Ubon which were deployed to Cam Ranh Bay and four A-1 aircraft deployed from Nakhon Phanom to Bien Hoa for SAR efforts.

The attack sortie surge in support of the Cambodian campaign peaked during the second week in May to 4,336 sorties, 2,400 in-country and 1,936 in Cambodia (Fig. 18). This compared to a pre-Cambodian weekly average of 2,850 sorties in 1970 and 3,150 in 1969. The additional sorties were obtained by picking up the sorties from Da Nang, Phu Cat, and Tuy Hoa made available from the interdiction campaign in the STEEL TIGER area of southern Laos, because of the onset of the Southwest Monsoon, and by increasing the fighter aircraft utilization rates from pre-Cambodian levels of .75 - .80 sorties per day per aircraft to peak levels of 1.13 for F-4s, 1.38 for A-37s, and 1.44 for F-100s (Fig. 19).

The campaign did not affect air support for I Corps which actually increased about 200 sorties per week (Fig. 20). IV Corps support also continued at about the previous level. This was achieved by having USAF preplanned sorties fill in for the VNAF flights, most of

## SORTIE DISTRIBUTION

| | APRIL | | | | MAY | | | | JUNE | | | |
|---|---|---|---|---|---|---|---|---|---|---|---|---|
| | 1-7 | 8-14 | 15-21 | 22-28 | 29-5 | 6-12 | 13-19 | 20-26 | 27-2 | 3-9 | 10-16 | 17-23 | 24-30 |
| I = IMMEDIATE  P = PREPLANNED | | | | | | I CORPS | | | | | | | |
| FREE WORLD - I | 169 | 221 | 275 | 178 | 366 | 375 | 202 | 336 | 327 | 318 | 148 | 217 | 142 |
| FREE WORLD - P | 740 | 710 | 613 | 623 | 627 | 779 | 665 | 647 | 667 | 734 | 645 | 660 | 650 |
| VNAF | 80 | 122 | 147 | 81 | 118 | 142 | 156 | 146 | 156 | 140 | 104 | 122 | 138 |
| TOTAL | 989 | 1053 | 1035 | 882 | 1111 | 1296 | 1023 | 1129 | 1150 | 1192 | 897 | 999 | 930 |
| | | | | | | II CORPS | | | | | | | |
| FREE WORLD - I | 566 | 662 | 429 | 443 | 267 | 162 | 170 | 135 | 123 | 117 | 121 | 104 | 184 |
| FREE WORLD - P | 128 | 182 | 258 | 279 | 161 | 199 | 103 | 142 | 222 | 230 | 173 | 175 | 189 |
| VNAF | 141 | 143 | 127 | 148 | 93 | 8 | - | 36 | 10 | 27 | 68 | 44 | 81 |
| TOTAL | 835 | 987 | 814 | 870 | 521 | 369 | 273 | 313 | 355 | 374 | 362 | 323 | 454 |
| | | | | | | III CORPS | | | | | | | |
| FREE WORLD - I | 140 | 192 | 160 | 193 | 89 | 63 | 29 | 54 | 70 | 52 | 30 | 24 | 80 |
| FREE WORLD - P | 371 | 226 | 250 | 305 | 351 | 223 | 203 | 329 | 226 | 180 | 250 | 169 | 181 |
| VNAF | 377 | 381 | 320 | 279 | 138 | 134 | 99 | 90 | 85 | 207 | 146 | 122 | 139 |
| TOTAL | 888 | 799 | 730 | 777 | 578 | 420 | 331 | 473 | 381 | 439 | 426 | 315 | 400 |
| | | | | | | IV CORPS | | | | | | | |
| FREE WORLD - I | 50 | 82 | 76 | 92 | 62 | 66 | 42 | 64 | 56 | 49 | 80 | 50 | 58 |
| FREE WORLD - P | 112 | 40 | 36 | 77 | 129 | 111 | 111 | 173 | 164 | 198 | 170 | 160 | 190 |
| VNAF | 222 | 242 | 255 | 296 | 136 | 138 | 63 | 46 | 61 | 141 | 94 | 109 | 140 |
| TOTAL | 384 | 364 | 367 | 465 | 327 | 315 | 216 | 283 | 281 | 388 | 344 | 319 | 388 |
| | | | | | | TOTAL IN-COUNTRY | | | | | | | |
| FREE WORLD | 2276 | 2315 | 2097 | 2190 | 2052 | 1978 | 1525 | 1880 | 1855 | 1878 | 1617 | 1558 | 1674 |
| VNAF | 820 | 888 | 849 | 804 | 485 | 422 | 318 | 318 | 312 | 515 | 412 | 397 | 498 |
| | | | | | | CAMBODIA | | | | | | | |
| FREE WORLD - I | | | | | 159 | 359 | 155 | 351 | 248 | 278 | 177 | 310 | 266 |
| FREE WORLD - P | | | | | 595 | 1134 | 698 | 879 | 561 | 452 | 472 | 494 | 978 |
| VNAF | | | | | 375 | 443 | 374 | 326 | 450 | 272 | 284 | 234 | 287 |
| TOTAL | | | | | 1129 | 1936 | 1227 | 1556 | 1259 | 1102 | 933 | 1038 | 1131 |
| | | | | | | LAOS | | | | | | | |
| FREE WORLD | 2392 | 2457 | 2406 | 2226 | 1961 | 2019 | 1607 | 1791 | 1563 | 1372 | 944 | 826 | 943 |

SOURCE: TACC BRIEFING NOTES

FIGURE 18

## AIRCRAFT UTILIZATION

| | 1-7 | 8-14 | 15-21 | 22-28 | 29-5 | 6-12 | 13-19 | 20-26 | 27-2 | 3-9 | 10-16 | 17-23 | 24-30 |
|---|---|---|---|---|---|---|---|---|---|---|---|---|---|
| 3 TFW (F100) | .95 | 1.00 | .95 | .94 | 1.24 | 1.44 | .84 | 1.06 | .77 | .83 | .78 | .90 | Dis-banded |
| 31 TFW | .76 | .88 | .89 | .79 | .97 | .89 | .71 | .90 | .81 | .92 | .75 | .76 | .94 |
| 35 TFW | .80 | .93 | .87 | .82 | 1.03 | 1.08 | .81 | 1.13 | .93 | .94 | .67 | .64 | .95 |
| 366 TFW | .70 | .70 | .91 | .66 | .80 | 1.05 | .79 | .86 | .90 | .88 | .65 | .78 | .93 |
| 12 TFW | 1.31 | 1.16 | .90 | 1.03 | .92 | .94 | .81 | .97 | .90 | .97 | .66 | .84 | 1.12 |
| 3 TFW (A-37) | .87 | .82 | .80 | .89 | 1.20 | 1.38 | .98 | 1.28 | .89 | .95 | .74 | .83 | 1.02 |
| TOTAL | .85 | .89 | .87 | .83 | 1.03 | 1.09 | .82 | 1.04 | .89 | .93 | .71 | .77 | .98 |

| | 1-7 | 8-14 | 15-21 | 22-28 | 29-5 | 6-12 | 13-19 | 20-26 | 27-2 | 3-9 | 10-16 | 17-23 | 24-30 |
|---|---|---|---|---|---|---|---|---|---|---|---|---|---|
| USMC | 1.15 | 1.20 | 1.20 | 1.22 | 1.37 | 1.68 | .96 | 1.33 | 1.01 | 1.10 | .98 | N/A | N/A |
| RAAF | 1.00 | 1.00 | 1.00 | 1.10 | 1.03 | 1.10 | 1.00 | 1.10 | 1.12 | 1.12 | 1.00 | N/A | N/A |

SOURCE: TACC BRIEFING NOTES

FIGURE 19

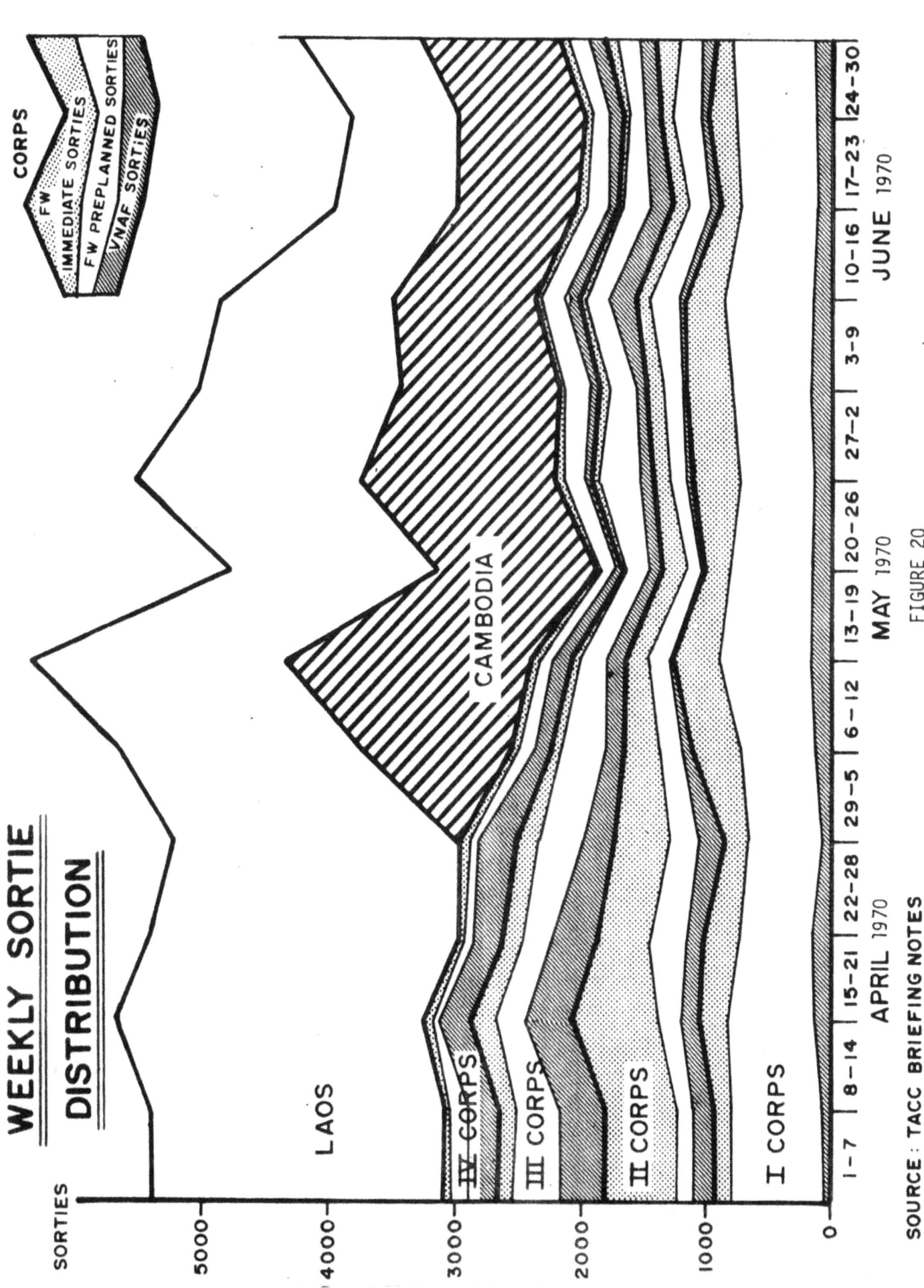

which diverted to Cambodia. Although the preplanned sorties remained at about previous levels in II and III Corps, the total number of sorties in these corps dropped by more than half. The cause was the shifting of most of the VNAF sorties and USAF immediate sorties into Cambodia along with the ground forces.

Tactical air operations in Cambodia began on 29 April 1970 with VANF fighter aircraft flying 166 sorties in support of TOAN THANG 42 in the Parrot's Beak. The VNAF continued to supply the bulk of the support as USAF aircraft flew only 310 sorties compared to 1,604 by the VNAF (Fig. 11). For TOAN THANG 43 in the FISHHOOK, however, USAF aircraft flew 3,000 sorties and the VNAF 364. This pattern held true for the other operations with USAF aircraft supplying nearly all of the support in areas adjacent to II and III Corps and the VNAF providing the major support for TAN THANG 42 and areas adjacent to IV Corps (Figs. 11, 13-16). In addition to the 754 USAF and 374 VNAF fighter sorties flown during the first week, 27 USAF gunship and six flareship missions provided night support which continued throughout the campaign. The first psychological warfare (psywar) missions started on 3 May, and during the same week COMMANDO VAULT missions cleared four helicopter landing zones with 15,000-lb. BLU-82 bombs.

The peak effort of the entire campaign came in the second week (6-12 May) as ground forces launched four operations--TOAN THANG 44, 45, 500, CUU LONG I--and increased activity in BINH TAY I which had begun on 5 May. In addition to 1,936 USAF and VNAF fighter sorties, 71 USAF and 32 VNAF gunships flew missions in Cambodia.

The number of airstrikes dropped off the third week as TOAN THANG 44 and 500 ended and activity decreased in the FISHHOOK and Parrot's Beak. Sorties surged again the next week (20 - 26 May) when improved weather brought increased activity in all of the areas and BINH TAY III was launched. Airstrikes in support of ground forces declined steadily as certain operations terminated at the end of May and troops concentrated on clearing out the caches through June.

The USAF delivered 20 COMMANDO VAULT helicopter landing zone (HLZ) weapons in support of the cross-border operations (Fig. 22). Sixteen of these deliveries resulted in usable HLZ areas--nine one-ship areas, six two-ship, and one three-ship. Dropped by parachute extraction from a C-130 between 6,000 and 12,000 feet above ground level, the COMMANDO VAULT weapon, either a 10,000-lb. M-121 or 15,000-lb. BLU-82 bomb, was fuze-extended to detonate about three feet above ground level. The resulting blast cleared the jungle canopy out to a 60-meter radius. Delivery of the instant HLZ weapons was done by specially trained crews of the 463d Tactical Airlift Wing, Clark AB, Philippines, who operated out of Cam Ranh Bay.

Of the four COMMANDO VAULT deliveries which failed to provide a landing zone, one bomb fell 2,500 meters from the desired point of impact and another landed on sloping terrain unsuitable for an HLZ. One bomb failed to separate from its launching platform and landed as

Helicopter Landing Zone preparation.
FIGURE 21

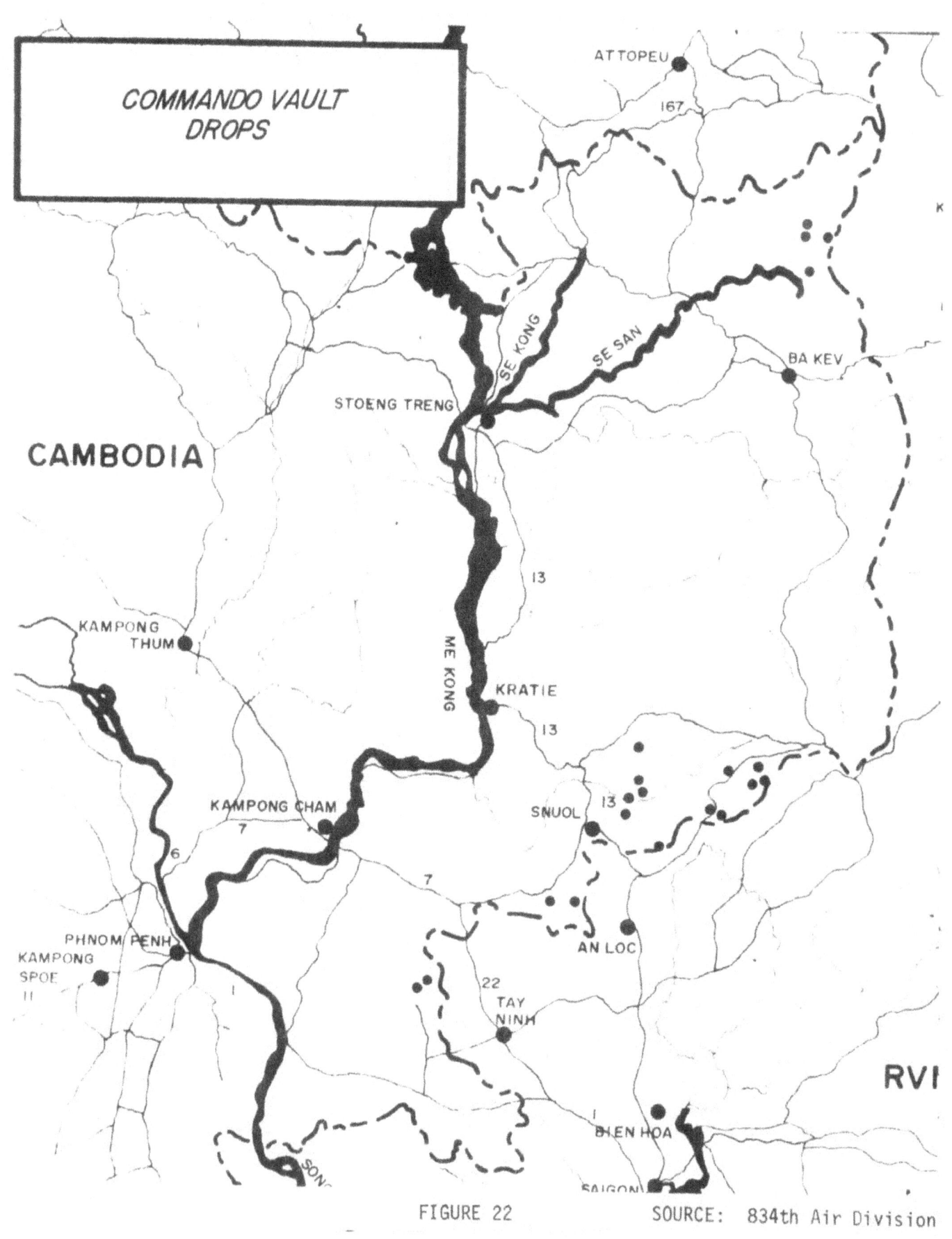

FIGURE 22      SOURCE: 834th Air Division

## BOMB DAMAGE ASSESSMENT BY OPERATION

| | TT-42 DEST/DAM | TT-43 DEST/DAM | TT-44 DEST/DAM | TT-45 DEST/DAM | TT-46 DEST/DAM | PT-I DEST/DAM | PT-II DEST/DAM | PT-III DEST/DAM | CL-I DEST/DAM | CL-II DES/DAM | CL-III DEST/DAM | TOTAL DEST/DAM |
|---|---|---|---|---|---|---|---|---|---|---|---|---|
| KILLED BY AIR | 464 / 554 | 218 / 57 | 53 / 0 | 63 / 6 | 9 / 56 | 42 / 21 | 32 / 40 | 20 / 20 | 0 / 467 | 25 / — | 0 / 80 | 926 / 1358 |
| STRUCTURES | 2789 / 211 | 1044 / 74 | 317 / 48 | 536 / 91 | 47 / 0 | 432 / 39 | 128 / 10 | 159 / 48 | 471 / 198 | 138 / 62 | 208 / 127 | 6269 / 913 |
| BUNKERS | 1645 / 175 | 1972 / 350 | 344 / 52 | 678 / 120 | 72 / 36 | 250 / 41 | 53 / 0 | 54 / 1 | 46 / 39 | 103 / 9 | 53 / 38 | 5270 / 861 |
| SEC FIRE/EXP | 31 / 34 | 207 / 84 | 179 / 21 | 67 / 21 | 12 / 3 | 61 / 55 | 17 / 48 | 12 / 21 | 0 / 5 | 5 / 2 | 0 / 0 | 591 / 294 |
| VEHICLES | 18 / 0 | 14 / 2 | 0 / 1 | 15 / 14 | 3 / 0 | 3 / 1 | 2 / 0 | 8 / 3 | 0 / 1 | 0 / 0 | 0 / 0 | 63 / 22 |
| FOR POSITIONS | 563 / 142 | 289 / 25 | 31 / 11 | 28 / 4 | 8 / 0 | 0 / 0 | 0 / 0 | 0 / 0 | 5 / 0 | 0 / 0 | 0 / 0 | 924 / 182 |
| ROADS | 0 / 0 | 2 / 0 | 0 / 0 | 24 / 0 | 0 / 0 | 0 / 0 | 0 / 0 | 2 / 0 | 0 / 0 | 1 / 0 | 0 / 0 | 29 / 0 |
| BRIDGES | 4 / 0 | 7 / 2 | 2 / 0 | 12 / 9 | 6 / 4 | 14 / 1 | 1 / 0 | 4 / 1 | 0 / 0 | 0 / 0 | 0 / 0 | 50 / 17 |
| WATER BUFFALO | 2 / 0 | 0 / 0 | 0 / 0 | 0 / 0 | 0 / 0 | 11 / 0 | 38 / 0 | 0 / 0 | 7 / 0 | 0 / 0 | 0 / 0 | 58 / 0 |
| WAREHOUSES | 0 / 0 | 0 / 0 | 0 / 0 | 0 / 0 | 0 / 0 | 4 / 0 | 0 / 0 | 0 / 0 | 0 / 0 | 0 / 0 | 0 / 0 | 4 / 0 |
| AUTO WPN POSITIONS | 17 / 2 | 3 / 1 | 1 / 0 | 7 / 0 | 1 / 0 | 1 / 3 | 1 / 1 | 0 / 0 | 0 / 0 | 7 / 0 | 0 / 0 | 38 / 7 |
| AMMUNITION | 0 / 0 | 0 / 0 | 0 / 0 | 2 / 0 | 1 / 0 | 0 / 0 | 0 / 0 | 0 / 0 | 0 / 0 | 0 / 0 | 0 / 0 | 3 / 0 |
| RICE (TONS) | 1 / 0 | 41 / 0 | 0 / 0 | 0 / 0 | 0 / 0 | 0 / 0 | 0 / 0 | 0 / 0 | 0 / 0 | 0 / 0 | 0 / 0 | 42 / 0 |
| POL DRUMS | 2 / 0 | 0 / 0 | 0 / 0 | 36 / 25 | 0 / 0 | 0 / 0 | 0 / 0 | 3 / 0 | 0 / 0 | 0 / 0 | 0 / 0 | 41 / 25 |
| MOTOR CYCLES | 0 / 0 | 0 / 0 | 2 / 0 | 0 / 0 | 0 / 0 | 0 / 0 | 0 / 0 | 0 / 0 | 0 / 0 | 0 / 0 | 0 / 0 | 2 / 0 |
| FOOD CACHES | 0 / 0 | 1 / 0 | 0 / 0 | 0 / 0 | 0 / 0 | 0 / 0 | 0 / 0 | 3 / 0 | 0 / 0 | 0 / 0 | 0 / 0 | 4 / 0 |
| CAVES | 0 / 0 | 0 / 0 | 0 / 0 | 0 / 2 | 0 / 0 | 66 / 0 | 0 / 0 | 16 / 0 | 0 / 0 | 0 / 0 | 0 / 0 | 82 / 2 |
| RICE CACHES (NO.) | 0 / 0 | 2 / 0 | 0 / 0 | 2 / 0 | 0 / 0 | 0 / 0 | 0 / 0 | 0 / 0 | 0 / 0 | 0 / 0 | 0 / 0 | 4 / 0 |
| TRAIL CUTS | 1 / 0 | 1 / 0 | 0 / 0 | 0 / 0 | 8 / 0 | 0 / 0 | 1 / 0 | 25 / 0 | 0 / 0 | 0 / 0 | 0 / 0 | 36 / 0 |
| CASES MEDICINE | 0 / 0 | 0 / 0 | 0 / 0 | 0 / 0 | 0 / 0 | 0 / 0 | 17 / 0 | 0 / 0 | 0 / 0 | 0 / 0 | 0 / 0 | 17 / 0 |
| FOX HOLES | 115 / 0 | 0 / 0 | 0 / 0 | 0 / 0 | 0 / 0 | 10 / 0 | 33 / 15 | 21 / 2 | 10 / 0 | 14 / 3 | 0 / 0 | 203 / 20 |
| GUN POSITIONS | 75 / 0 | 0 / 0 | 0 / 0 | 0 / 0 | 0 / 0 | 0 / 0 | 0 / 0 | 0 / 0 | 0 / 0 | 0 / 0 | 0 / 0 | 75 / 0 |
| SAMPANS | 5 / 0 | 1 / 0 | 0 / 0 | 1 / 0 | 0 / 0 | 1 / 0 | 0 / 0 | 0 / 0 | 69 / 0 | 0 / 0 | 0 / 0 | 77 / 0 |
| WELLS | 0 / 0 | 2 / 0 | 0 / 0 | 2 / 0 | 0 / 0 | 0 / 0 | 0 / 0 | 0 / 0 | 0 / 0 | 0 / 0 | 0 / 0 | 0 / 0 |

SOURCE: TACC Briefing Notes

FIGURE 23

## ORDNANCE DELIVERED

| | USAF | VNAF | | USAF | VNAF |
|---|---|---|---|---|---|
| BLU1B FIRE BMB | 1834 | | MK 82 GPB72FUS | 40 | |
| BLU10B FIRE BMB | 4 | | MK82HDGPB | 16,262 | |
| BLU27 FIRE BMB | 4798 | | MK36 GPB 500 | 1,057 | |
| BLU32B FIRE BMB | 2427 | | M117 GPB 750 | 1,317 | 318 |
| CBU12 INC SMK | 2 | | M117HDGPB 750 | 496 | |
| CBU22 | 14 | | M117 GPB36FUSE | 239 | |
| CBU19 RIOT CTL | 4 | | MK83 GPB 1000 | 8 | |
| CBU24 AN PR/MT | 669 | | MK84 GPB 2000 | 85 | |
| CBU25 AN PR/MT | 751 | | MK84 GPBKMU35 | 2 | |
| CBU42 WAAPM | 2 | | M47S SMK BOMB | 148 | |
| CBU46 ANTI MAT | 229 | | M35 INC CLS | 8 | |
| CBU46 ANTI PER | 6 | | M36 INC CLS | 3 | |
| CBU49 | 252 | | MLU10B AIR MINE | 143 | |
| LAU3 RKT LNCH | 1771 | 416 | AGM-12 BULLPUP | 4 | |
| LAU59 RKT LNCH | 9 | | AIM-7 SPARROW | 4 | |
| MK81 GPB 250 | 8 | 48 | ADU272 DISPENSER | 91 | |
| MK82 GPB 500 | 12325 | 5907 | ADU253 DISPENSER | 20 | |
| MK82 GPB18FUS | 68 | | MK-77 NAPALM | | 64 |
| MK82 GPB36FUS | 164 | | CBU39 | | 14 |

## ARC LIGHT SUMMARY

| BDA | | | | SORTIES | |
|---|---|---|---|---|---|
| KIA | 194 | FIGHT POS | 133 | BINH TAY I | 47 |
| WIA | 28 | BUNKERS | 2031 | BINH TAY III | 24 |
| BRIDGES | 8 | STRUCTURES | 504 | TOAN THANG 45/46 | 218 |
| CREW WPNS | 5 | TRENCH | 1437 | TOAN THANG 43 | 323 |
| POL | 18 | SEC EXP | 1001 | TOAN THANG 44 | 18 |
| HUTS | 93 | RICE CACHES | 4 | CUU LONG II | 23 |
| LOC | 17 | AMMO CACHES | 217 | | |
| TUNNELS | 19 | WPNS CACHES | 276 | TOTAL | 653 |
| VEHICLES | 90 | | | | |

FIGURE 24

a dud. The fourth failure resulted from detonation at treetop level, well above the optimum burst height.[23/]

By 30 June, all U.S. ground operations had ceased and after 1 July only CUU LONG III continued with VNAF support. In support of the cross-border campaign, USAF aircraft flew 5,189 preplanned and 1,675 immediate airstrike sorties as well as 193 gunship and 44 flareship missions. The VNAF flew 2,691 strike sorties and 184 gunship missions. The bomb damage included 926 confirmed and 1,358 probable KBA, 6,269 structures and 5,270 bunkers destroyed, 50 bridges destroyed, and numerous other items (Fig. 23).

In addition to the tactical air support provided, B-52 ARC LIGHT missions flew 653 sorties in support of six of the twelve operations in Cambodia (Fig. 24). ARC LIGHT airstrikes provided massive firepower for LZ and objective preparations prior to initial combat assaults into each of these areas. B-52 missions were then targeted against suspected COSVN headquarters and other enemy locations beyond the 30-kilometer limitation for U.S. ground forces as shown in Fig. 9.

## Campaign Results

Except for some initial heavy contacts during TOAN THANG 42 in the Parrot's Beak and Binh Tay I and II in Base Areas 701 and 702, all operations were characterized by light contacts with scattered enemy units. Intelligence indicated that COSVN elements received up to several days' warning, although subordinate units were alerted only a few hours in advance. All of the main VC/NVA forces retreated into the interior of Cambodia, leaving only small suicide blocking forces and elements of rear service units behind. Evidence indicated that a few units split up into small groups and infiltrated into RVN behind the attacking forces.[24/]

Retreat of the enemy allowed friendly ground forces to sweep through the base areas with only 1,147 killed in action, compared to 11,562 enemy losses. These odds would likely have been much less favorable had tactical air not been available to coerce the enemy from his fortified defenses. His past experience with Allied tactical air was undoubtedly a major factor in his decision to withdraw. Thus the threat as well as the employment of airpower contributed to the ground forces' ability to advance rapidly enough to uncover the numerous caches and exploit these caches relatively unmolested.

The extensive storage areas discovered in the sanctuary bases far exceeded the estimates made by CICV Logistics Section prior to the campaign (Figs. 4, 26). Among the supplies captured were: (1) rice to feed 37,798 enemy soldiers for one year at reduced ration (1 lb. per day); (2) individual weapons to equip 55 full strength VC infantry battalions; (3) crew-served weapons to equip 33 full strength VC infantry battalions; and (4) mortar, rocket, and recoilless rifle rounds to sustain 18,585 enemy attacks by fire.

Of the 204 significant caches uncovered (Fig. 26), three of the

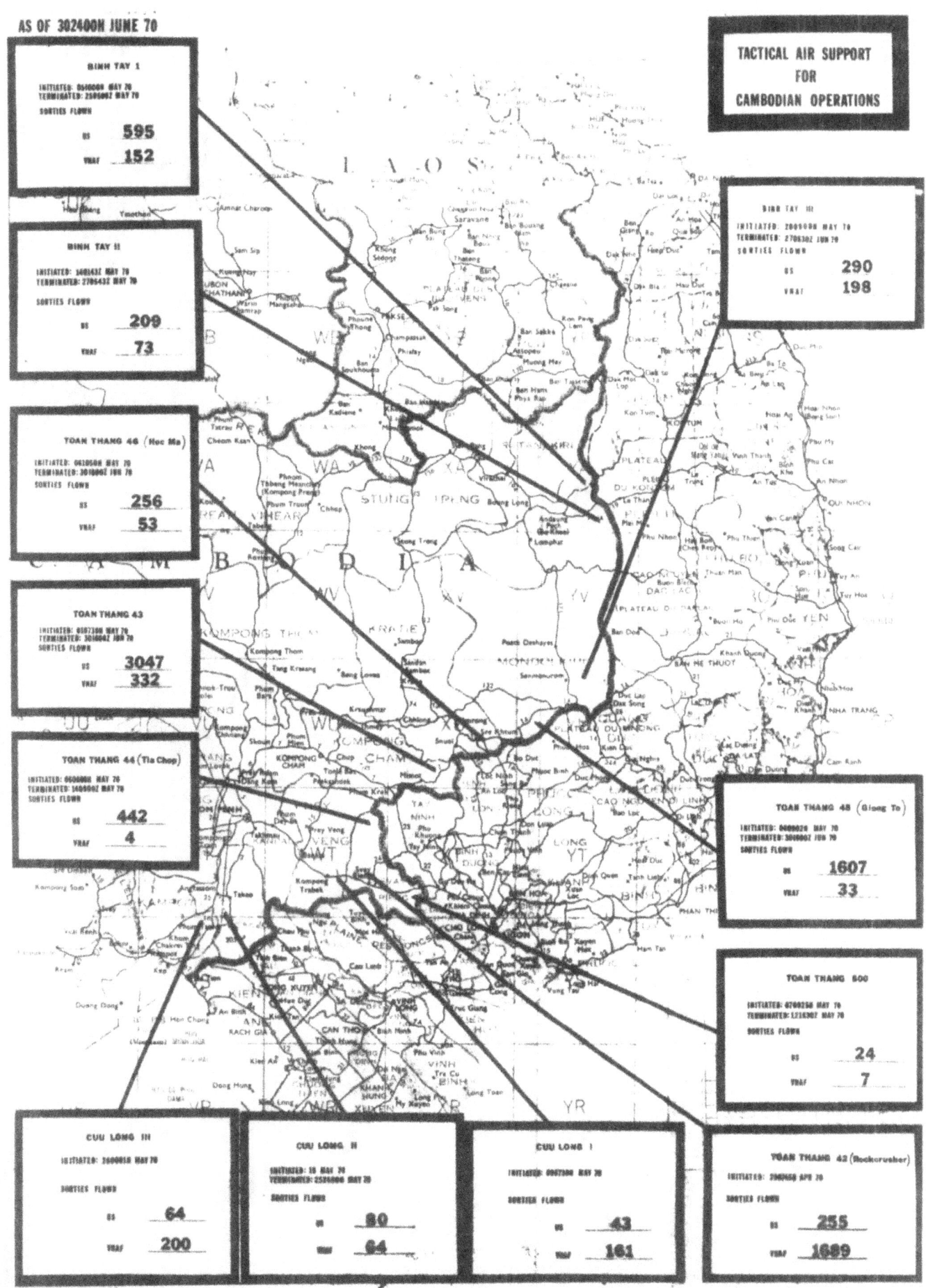

FIGURE 25

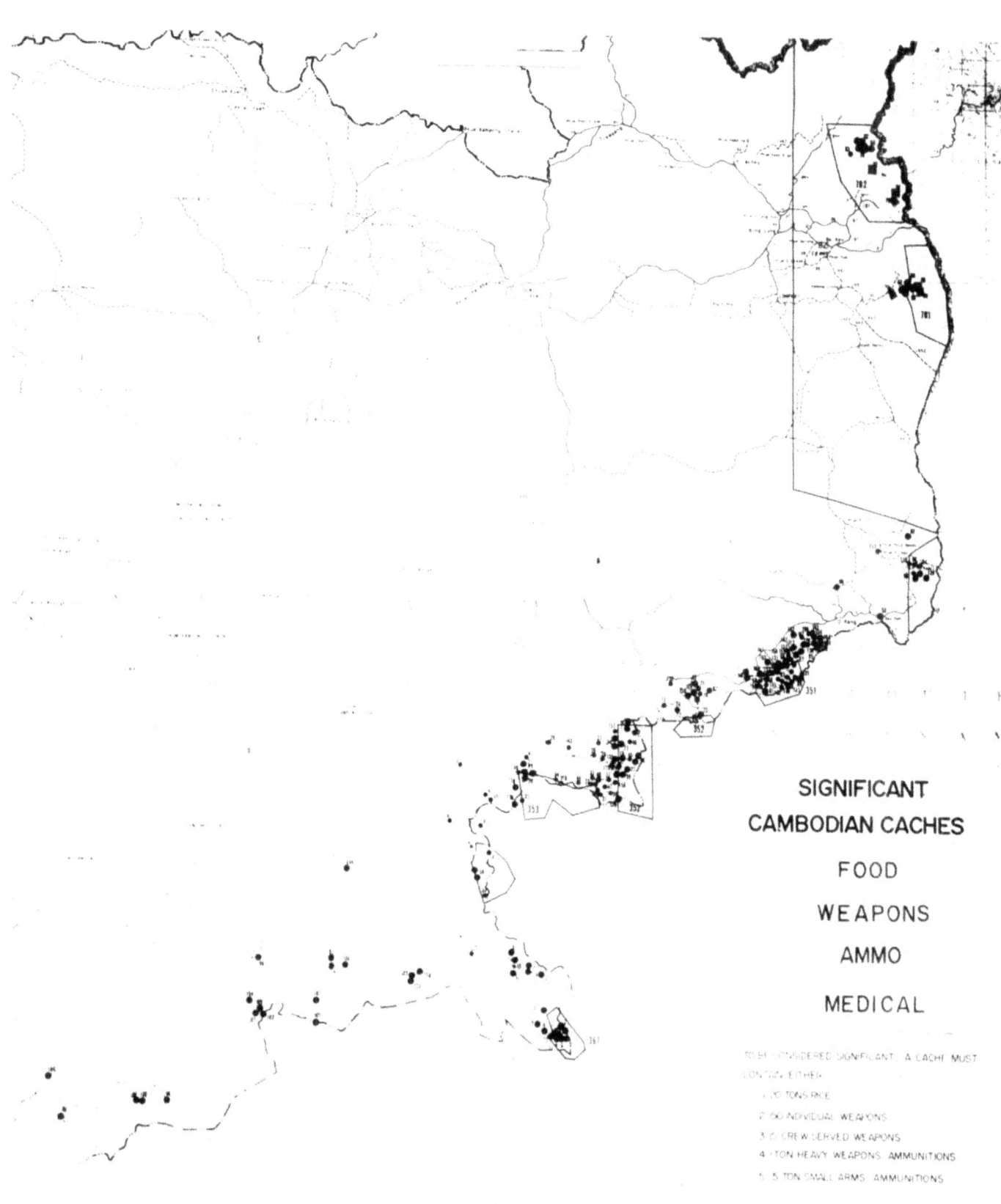

FIGURE 26

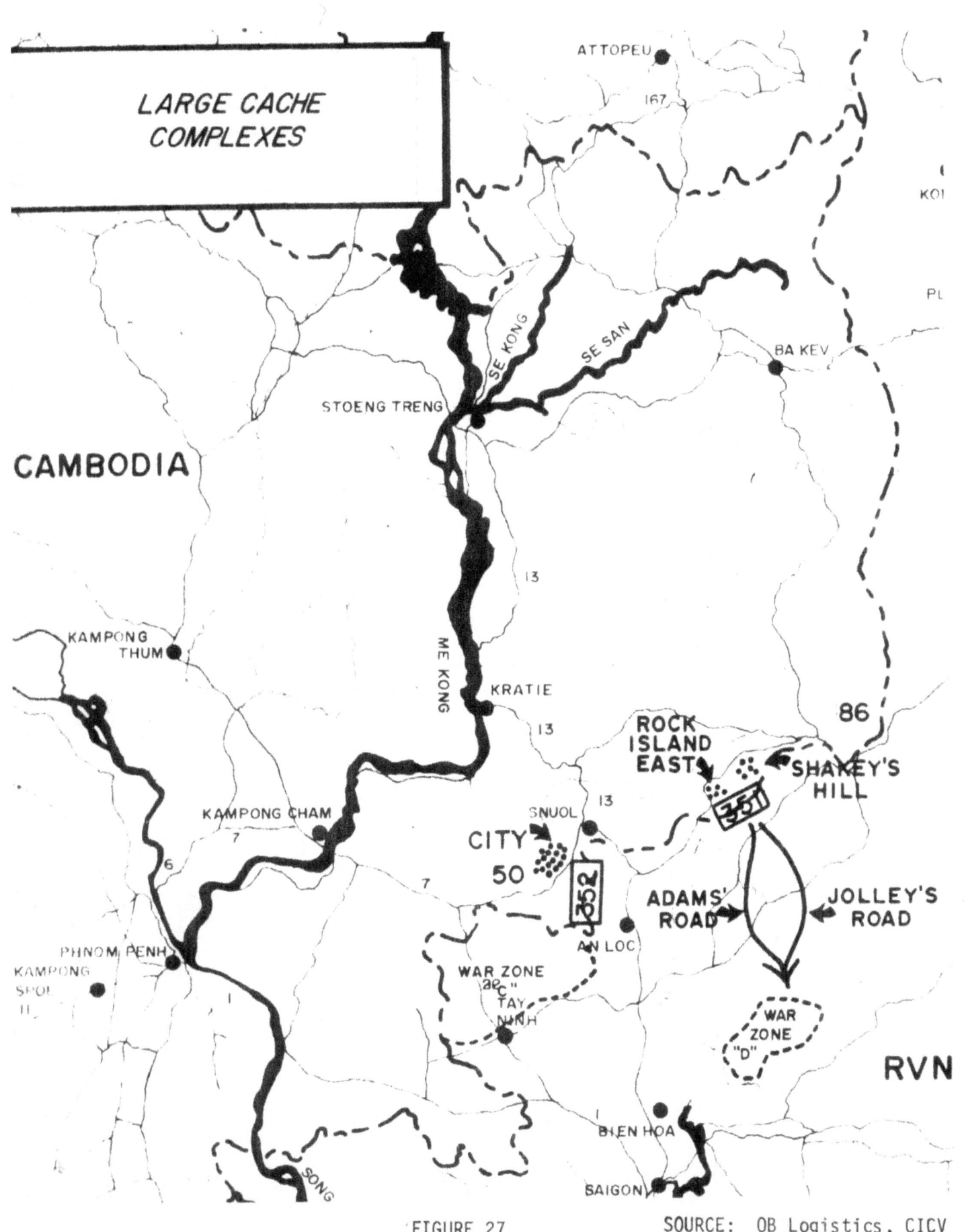

FIGURE 27

SOURCE: OB Logistics, CICV

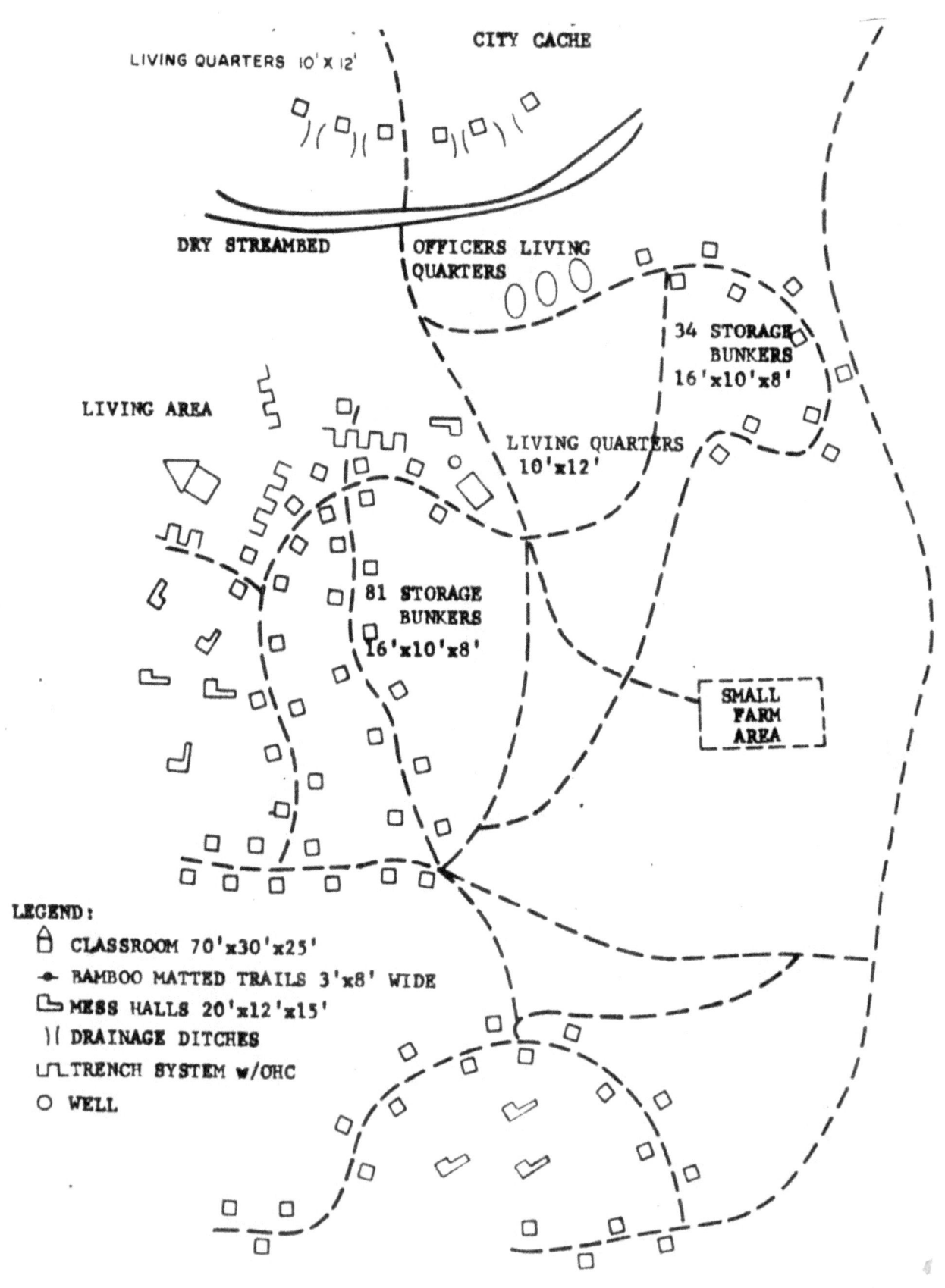

SOURCE: II FFORCEV PERINTREP NO. 21-70
FIGURE 28

# ROCK ISLAND EAST CACHE

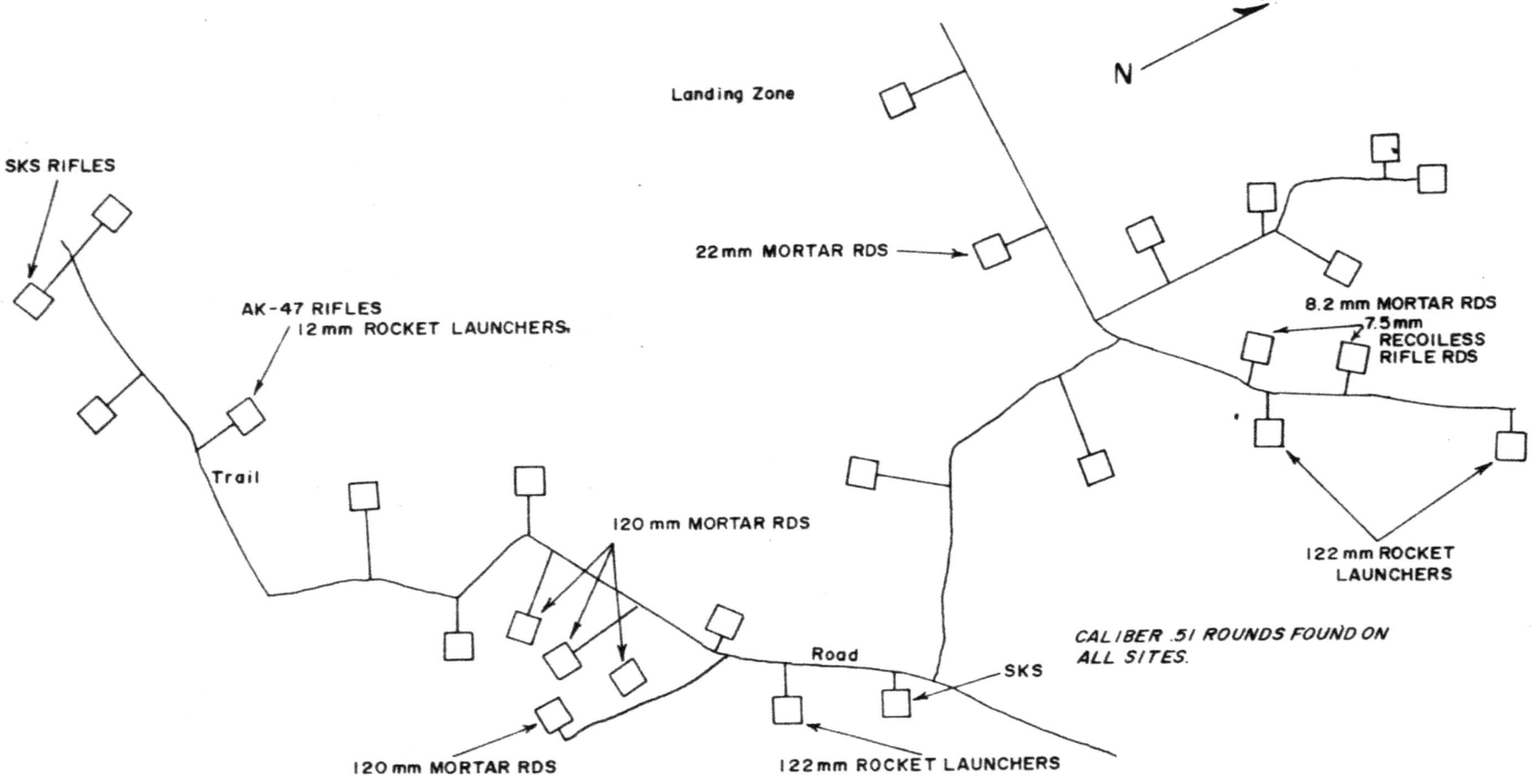

Landing Zone

22mm MORTAR RDS

8.2 mm MORTAR RDS
7.5mm RECOILLESS RIFLE RDS

122 mm ROCKET LAUNCHERS

CALIBER .51 ROUNDS FOUND ON ALL SITES.

SKS

Road

122 mm ROCKET LAUNCHERS

120 mm MORTAR RDS

120 mm MORTAR RDS

AK-47 RIFLES
12 mm ROCKET LAUNCHERS

Trail

SKS RIFLES

FIGURE 29

SOURCE: II FFORCEV PERINTREP NO. 21-70

largest cache complexes were discovered by elements of the 1st Air Cav Div in areas outside of the originally identified base areas (Fig. 27). On 4 May, elements of the 1st Air Cav Div discovered a large cache north of Base Area 352. It became well known as the "City." The complex contained a storage area and a training area (Fig. 28). The storage area contained 182 bunkers with more than 175 tons of supplies ranging from weapons and ammunition to bicycle tires. The bunkers were constructed both above and below ground and the camouflage varied from black plastic covered with brush to deeply dug bunkers covered with logs, earth, and brush. The entire area was covered by a dense forest canopy which prevented easy detection from the air.

"Rock Island East" cache was discovered on 8 May to the north of Base Area 351. Although not as well developed as the "City," it contained the greatest number of supplies with contents estimated at 330 tons. It was apparently a temporary transshipment point as the roads were unimproved and no attempt had been made to protect the supplies from the weather. They were stored at 28 individual sites and seemed to be sorted for loading on trucks (Fig. 29).

The most well-concealed complex was discovered by accident when Bravo Company, 5th Bn, 7th Cav came under attack while looking for a jungle highway. "Shakey's Hill," named after a Private First Class who was killed shortly after discovering it, contained 58 bunkers, or caves, tunneled deep into the hillside. They eventually disgorged approximately 170 tons of weapons and supplies.[25]

Based upon accepted enemy strengths prior to the start of the cross-border operations and estimates that the enemy desired to maintain six-month stocks of food and ammunition, the CICV Logistics Section estimated that Allied forces had captured the following percentages of the enemy's food and ammunition stockpiles:

| CATEGORY | AREA | CAPTURED (Tons) | PERCENT OF STOCKPILE |
|---|---|---|---|
| Food | No. II Corps | 683.3 | 65 |
| | So. II Corps and III, IV Corps | 6,193.0 | 129 |
| Ammo | No. II Corps | 40.6 | 09 |
| | So. II Corps and III, IV Corps | 1,761.4 | 81 |

The percentage of weapon stockpiles captured could not be adequately assessed, because even with sizable weapons losses within the RVN during the preceding two years, there had been no reports that indicated the enemy had faced any weapons shortages. It could only be concluded that considerable effort would be required to replace the large amount of weapons captured.

CICV Logistics personnel attempted to project the impact of the loss of these supplies on the enemy. CICV reasoned that as the VC/NVA were cut off from resupply by sea, they would have to expand their transportation system in the Laotian panhandle to meet southern RVN requirements. If the enemy could procure all of his food in Cambodia, his remaining requirements would still be about 5,000 tons a year for

Munitions found in complex.
FIGURE 30

Ammunition Stockpile.
FIGURE 31

southern RVN. Considering the distance from Laos to the using units and the need to replace his losses in Cambodia, the enemy's supply goal from Laos into northeastern Cambodia would be about 10,000 tons per year. To carry this increased load, the Lao logistic system would have to be expanded by roughly 50 percent. Although there were stockpiles available in the Laotian panhandle, shipment during the rainy season of even normal monthly ammunition requirements for southern RVN would tax the enemy's capabilities.

CICV Logistics therefore concluded the enemy would have difficulty maintaining his current requirements during the rainy season and could be expected to initiate a massive campaign to move supplies into Cambodia when the weather improved in November 1970. Because of the distance the material would have to travel, it would probably be February 1971 before these efforts would be felt in southern RVN. Thus, results of the cross-border operations had been to impair severely the enemy's logistic system, an effect he would feel for at least six to eight months.[26/]

CHAPTER III

INTERDICTION

## Enemy Offensive

While withdrawing from the Allied advance against his base areas in the border region, the enemy remained active in other parts of Cambodia (Fig. 32).[1] He initiated a westward thrust from northeast Cambodia toward the Mekong River and Phnom Penh, continued his efforts to isolate the capital by cutting the major LOCs, and increased his pressure on the government positions in the northeast.[2]

On 5-6 May 1970, the enemy captured Kratie on the Mekong. Kratie was the FANK ordnance depot for much of central Cambodia, and the supplies seized there partially offset some of the enemy losses in eastern Cambodia. After Kratie fell, two VC/NVA battalions turned north along the Mekong toward Stung Treng, about 125 kilometers away, and during the night of 14-15 May launched their attack. By 18 May, the city had fallen, giving the enemy control of the major LOCs north of Kratie. To further weaken FANK control in the north and northeast, enemy pressure was increased on Lomphat, Bakiev, and Labansiek. The first two were attacked on 14 May and almost nightly thereafter.

Enemy forces also exerted pressure south of Phnom Penh near Phum Banam and increased their activity near the provincial capital of Kampong Cham, about midway between Kratie and Phnom Penh. On 11-12 May, the

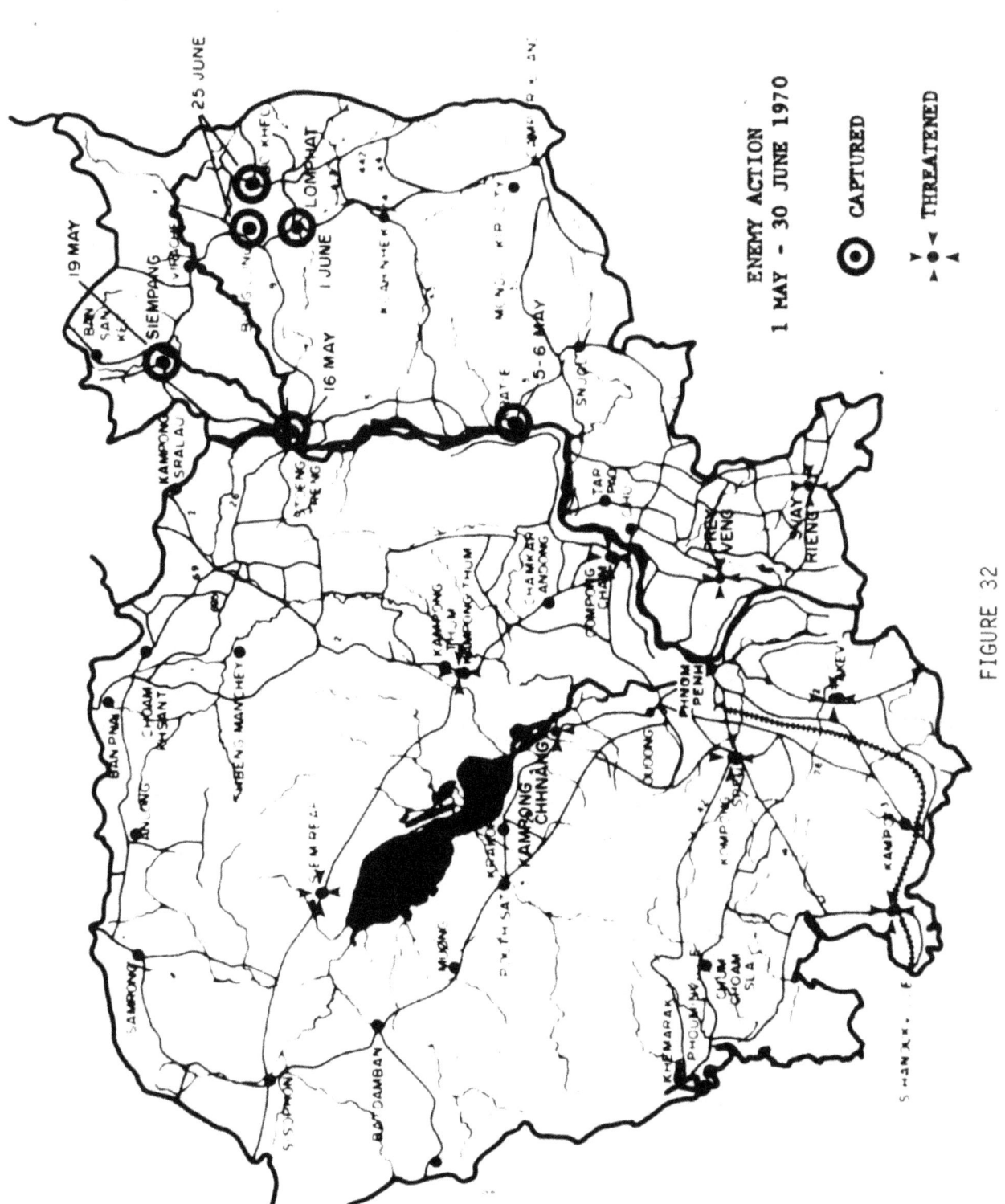

FIGURE 32

enemy captured Tonle Bet, just across the Mekong from Kampong Cham City. The Cambodian government reinforced Kampong Chan the same day. The city was attacked early on 15 May, and although the FANK forces remained in control, their families were evacuated the next day. Government forces retook Tonle Bet on 15 May, and on 18 May the FANK announced that all enemy forces had withdrawn from Kampong Cham.

In the northeast on the night of 20-21 May, both Lomphat and Labansiek were attacked. Both attacks were repulsed, but the situation, especially at the former location, continued to deteriorate. On 23 May, the enemy burned a key bridge on the road between the two towns, virtually cutting off Lomphat from all but air communication and supply. Labansiek was unsuccessfully attacked again on 24 May. Khmer troops reinforced the position on 26 May, and the siege was lifted. Lomphat, however, was reported surrounded on 26 May with the airfield in enemy hands. The deteriorating situation forced the defenders to withdraw to Labansiek on 31 May, leaving only it and Bakiev as significant government-controlled towns in the northeast. Since these two locations denied the enemy use of critical portions of Routes 19 and 194, his pressure against them continued.

Svay Rieng, in extreme southeast Cambodia, and Prey Veng, about midway between Svay Rieng and Phnom Penh, were also attacked on 26 and 28 May, respectively, by enemy forces, although neither was captured. West of the Mekong, enemy forces were increasingly noted in the vicinity of the critical provincial capital of Kampong Thom on Route 6. By controlling that city, the enemy would be able to seek the active aid of the 150,000 Vietnamese in the food-rich Tonle Sap area and also cut the Route 6 supply line into the northwest. On 30 May, Kampong Thom was reported isolated from the capital, and the next day it was struck by enemy mortar fire. The communist activity around Kampong Thom and the growing number of reports of enemy activity west of the Mekong signaled a change in communist objectives. In addition to controlling the LOCs east of the Mekong, the communists sought to topple Lon Nol's government.

Establishment of Interdiction Campaign

In early May, the Secretary of Defense (SECDEF) asked the CJCS for a transition plan from the Cambodian level of effort to that necessary to fulfill the strategic objectives in SEA.$^{3/}$ In response, the JCS submitted an outline plan for air interdiction operations in eastern Cambodia and on 16 May 1970 forwarded a copy to COMUSMACV for further planning. The plan was based on an intelligence estimate: (1) the enemy could be expected to attempt to consolidate his position in the northeastern provinces of Cambodia in preparation for renewed efforts in RVN; (2) closing of Cambodian ports would force the enemy to rely heavily on LOCs from Laos to maintain adequate logistical support of his forces in Cambodia and RVN; (3) increased use of Routes 13, 132, 14, 19, 194, 195, 1941, 1942, and the Mekong River and its tributaries; and (4) construction of new routes from Laos south into Cambodia could be anticipated.$^{4/}$

The mission stated in the plan was to maintain surveillance of enemy

PROPOSED INTERDICTION AREA

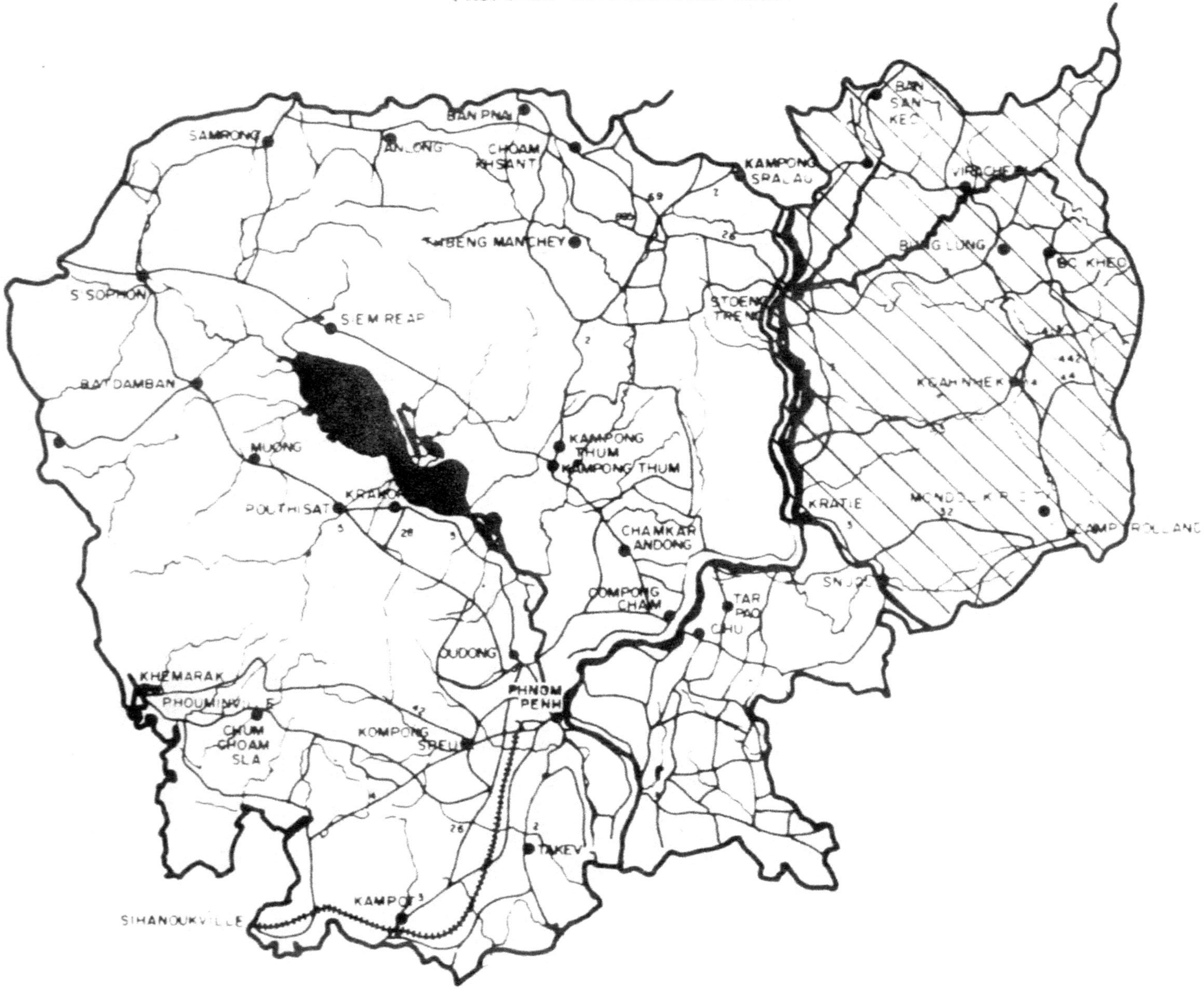

FIGURE 33

F-4 Airstrike
FIGURE 34

activities in Cambodia east of the Mekong River and to attack those activities as necessary to restrict enemy preparations for operations in Cambodia and RVN. The area of operations was defined as that portion in Cambodia east of a line 200 meters west of the Mekong River and north of Route 13 (Fig. 33). The tactical air operations outlined were viewed as an extension of the STEEL TIGER operations being conducted in Laos. The plan would use USAF forces then based in RVN and Thailand, and Navy aircraft from Task Force 77 for interdiction, air support of friendly troops in contact, and reconnaissance. ARC LIGHT strikes would be coordinated by COMUSMACV with approval for strikes requiring concurrence of the U.S. Embassy, Phnom Penh, and the Government of Cambodia (GOC). Restrictions for ARC LIGHT strikes were a minimum of one kilometer from the nearest noncombatants, not less than three kilometers from friendly combatants, and they were to avoid monuments, temples, and other cultural landmarks. Overall operating rules stated: (1) all targets and areas of operation had to be validated by the U.S. Ambassador, Phnom Penh, or his designated representative; (2) no operations could be conducted within the environs of Phnom Penh, unless specifically requested by the U.S. Embassy; (3) strikes had to be conducted under the control of an authorized FAC or using all-weather bombing systems, unless the U.S. Embassy authorized striking targets of opportunity; and (4) unless otherwise specified by the U.S. Embassy, fighter aircraft were authorized to strike any sites in Cambodia which fired at U.S. aircraft. The plan called for the U.S. Embassy, Phnom Penh, to coordinate operating areas, operating instructions, and target validations with the GOC.[5]

After receiving the JCS plan, 7AF representatives joined the J-3 staff at MACV to draft a proposal for air interdiction operations in Cambodia. They noted there was neither an identified LOC network similar to that in STEEL TIGER nor a corresponding logistics flow. Consequently, initial air support requirements would focus largely on support of friendly ground force operations (FANK or ARVN) but would include some interdiction. Implementation of the air interdiction program would require concentrated surveillance of the waterways and roads in northeastern Cambodia.

The draft proposed that to minimize U.S. involvement, requests for ARC LIGHT strikes, air support for ground forces, and interdiction strikes should pass directly from the National Forces of Cambodia (FANK) through Republic of Vietnam Armed Forces (RVNAF) channels to the TACC or MACV, as appropriate. Targets developed through all-source U.S. intelligence and recommendations for special operating areas would be passed to the VNAF for coordination with the FANK. Since the communications capability for fast coordination of air activities in special operating areas was not available, special Rules of Engagement (ROE) would have to be developed with GOC/FANK representatives.

The proposal stated that FAC procedures would be essentially the same as for in-country operations. The interdiction effort would be controlled exclusively by USAF FACs, while air support of ground forces could be controlled by USAF or VNAF FACs, dependent upon the source of air support. An exception to FAC procedures might be a requirement for a FANK observer to fly with a USAF FAC to overcome language difficulties. There would be a requirement to collocate a Tactical Air Control Party (TACP) and ALO with the FANK Combat Operations Center (COC). The VNAF was expected to be able to provide this support. Special Operating Areas were to be established with FANK concurrence and targets within these areas would be considered validated. Targets outside these areas would require case-by-case validation by the FANK. To implement the procedures, the draft proposed that the GVN arrange with the GOC for a coordination meeting between FANK, RVNAF, and MACV representatives in Saigon. COMUSMACV forwarded the proposal on 19 May 1970. 6/

The next day, the JCS informed COMUSMACV the proposal to provide air support for the FANK ground forces went beyond the authority anticipated for air operations in Cambodia. The VNAF could support the FANK within established guidelines, but any bonus effect for ground forces within Cambodia from U.S. air would have to come from interdiction operations. The JCS asked for a new proposal under these guidelines to include target identification procedures, methods to prevent noncombatant casualties, and the number of sorties anticipated. 7/

On 21 May 1970, COMUSMACV responded that air support for U.S. and ARVN forces through 30 June 1970 would continue as it was then being conducted and that air interdiction efforts would be directed against lucrative targets developed by reconnaissance flights. After 1 July 1970, air interdiction was to be conducted essentially as outlined on 19 May except for those portions of the proposal concerning close air support. The early establishment of special operating areas and close coordination with the FANK would be necessary to insure target identification procedures adequate to prevent noncombatant casualties. The use of FANK observers in USAF FAC aircraft to validate interdiction targets was considered the best procedure available. Some 52 interdiction targets had been identified and surveillance was continuing to determine which ones should be hit. Sortie levels through 1 July 1970 were estimated at approximately 100 per day, dropping after the withdrawal of U.S. ground forces to 50 per day.[8/]

On 24 May 1970, JCS replied with an execute message. The plan outlined in the message incorporated proposals made by COMUSMACV within the guidelines provided by JCS. It identified the area of operations as that part of Cambodia bounded by a line 200 meters west of the Mekong River on the west, the Laotian Border on the north, the South Vietnamese Border on the east, and Route 13 on the south (Fig. 35). Authority was granted to execute the plan as soon as necessary coordination could be made with the FANK and RVNAF.[9/]

Although the JCS plan conceived of the project as an extension of the STEEL TIGER operation, geography and past working relations with MACV dictated that operational direction was most logically a task for the TACC. The Deputy Director of the Tactical Air Control Center and his Chiefs of Plans and of Operations did the planning personally because of the close security imposed on the project.[10/] Plans for implementing the operation were basically completed after receiving the execute message on 24 May 1970.

40

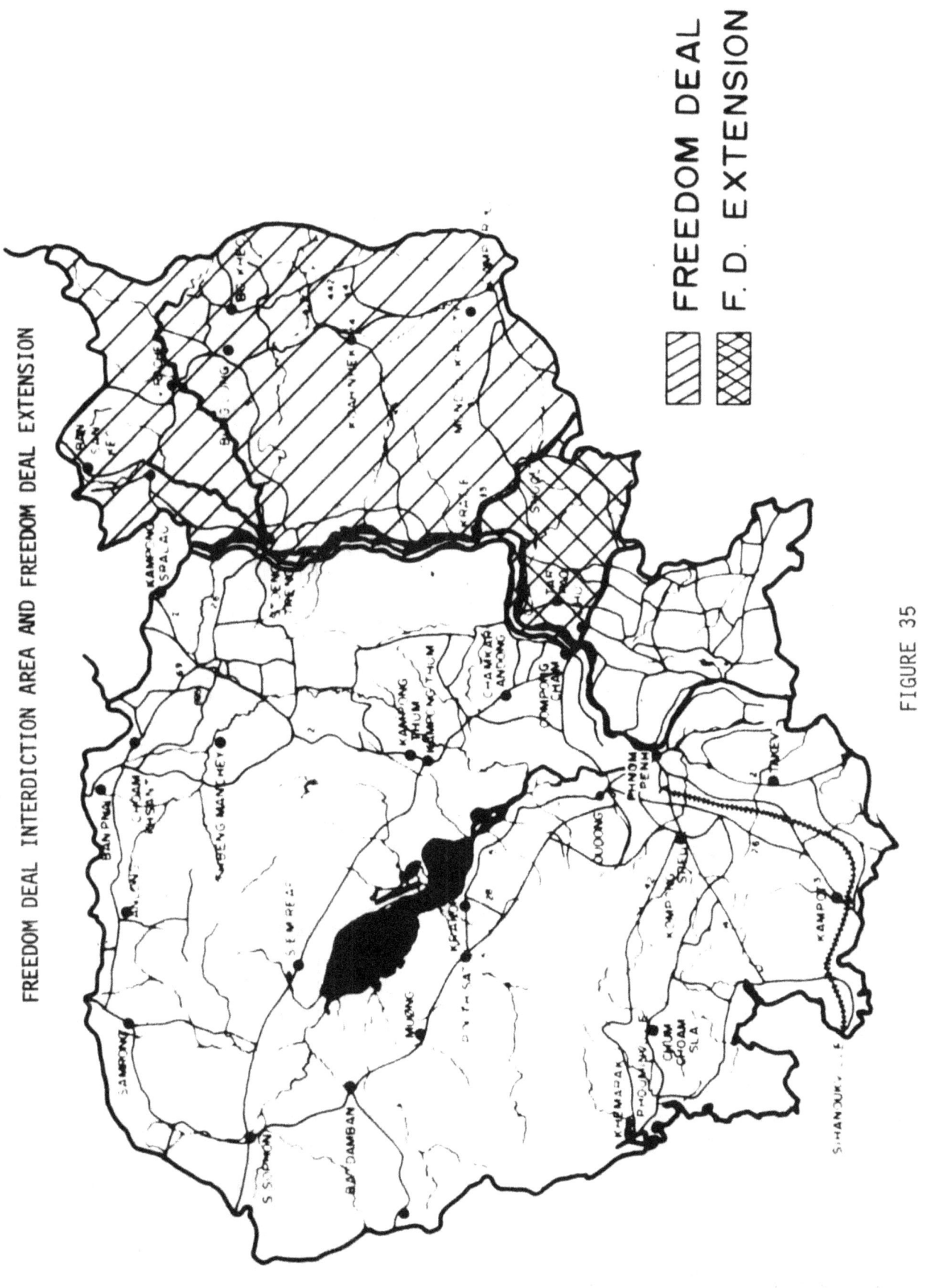

FIGURE 35

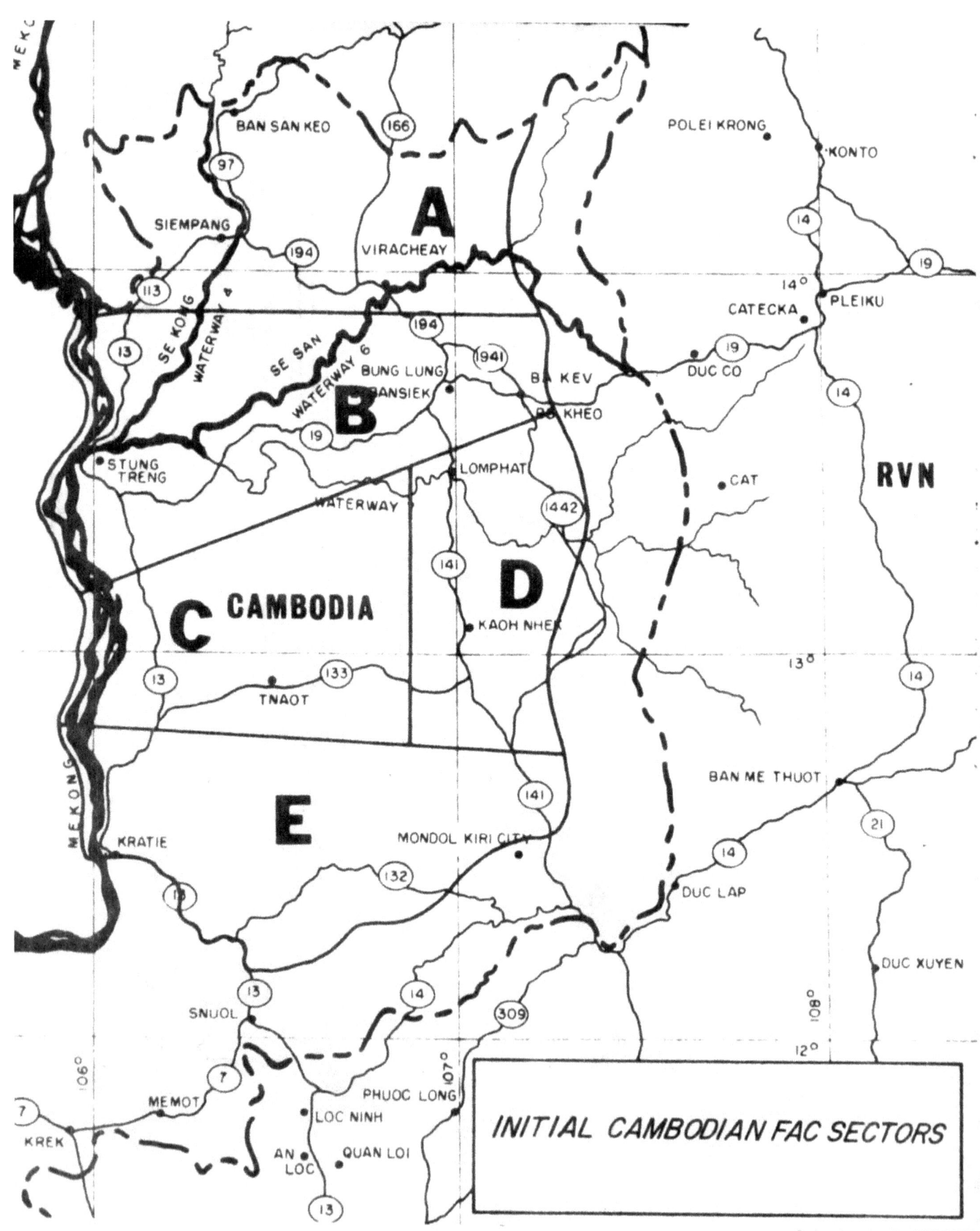

FIGURE 36

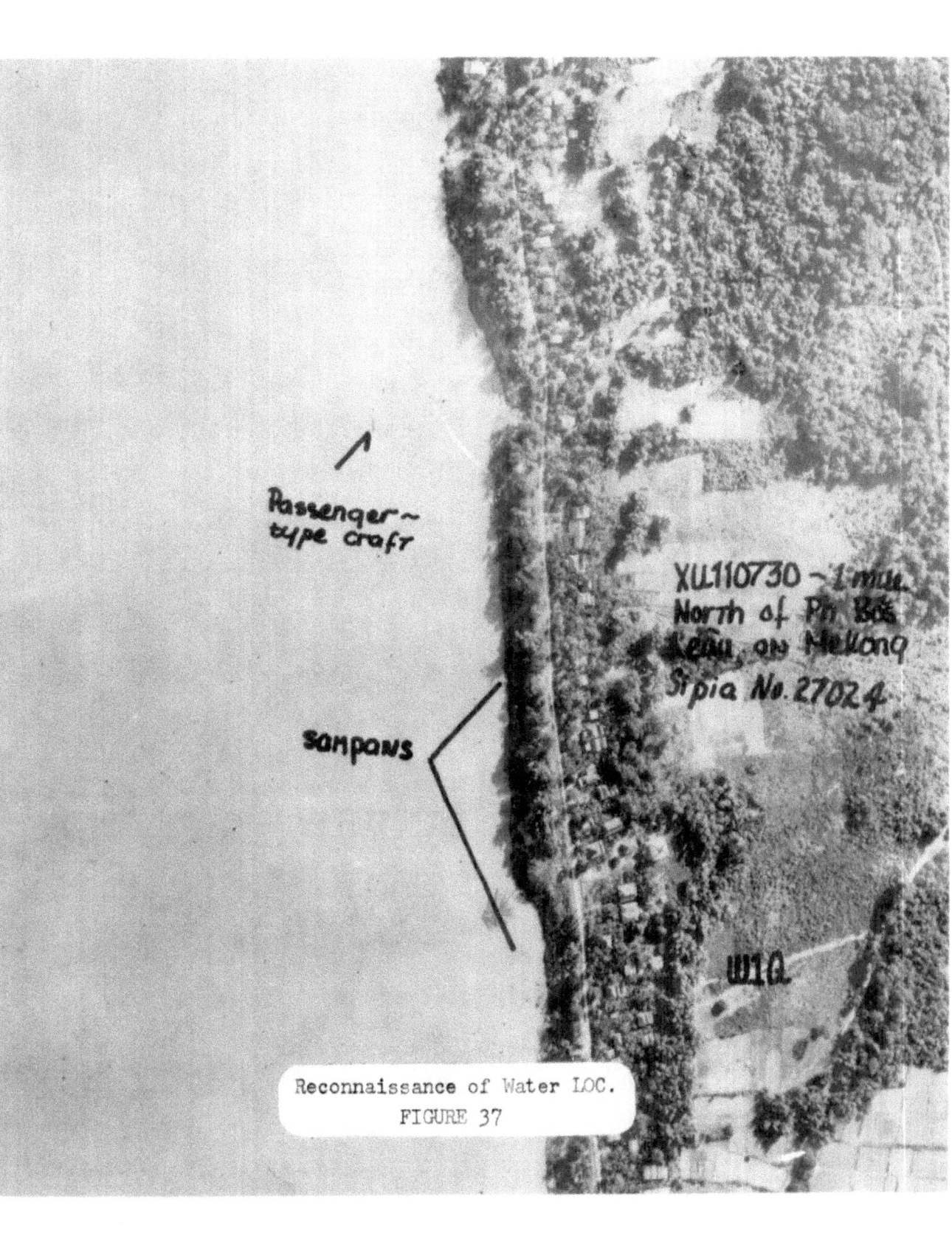

Reconnaissance of Water LOC.
FIGURE 37

Within four hours, a message went out from 7AF TACC tasking appropriate units to establish a special Cambodia LOC TACP at Pleiku AB. Manning for the TACP called for one ALO, seven FACs, five OV-10 aircraft, three radio operators, one Intelligence NCO, and one Administrative NCO. The ALO reported to the TACC for a detailed briefing and on 25 May, Eliot FACs started flying VR missions out of Pleiku AB.[11/]

On 25 May, the 7AF TACC tasked the fast-mover Stormy FACs flying F-4 aircraft out of Da Nang AB to provide three sorties per day. On 27 May, the TACC directed the 3d Tactical Fighter Wing (TFW) at Bien Hoa AB to fly three A-37 FAC sorties daily under the call sign Typhoon. Stormy FACs began flying VR missions on 27 May and Typhoon FACs on the 29th. Northeastern Cambodia was divided into five sectors with Stormy flying in the north, Eliot in the central area, and Typhoon in the south (Fig. 36). All VR reports were submitted by Flash message to 7AF TACC and Intelligence. Hand-held photography was processed on highest priority, annotated, and forwarded by courier.[12/] Provisions to assimilate the FAC reports with photo reconnaissance readouts and all-source intelligence were made on 21 May by establishing a Cambodian Task Force in the targeting division of 7AF Intelligence.[13/]

With provisions made for generating targets and directing airstrikes, all that remained was to work out details of coordination procedures and Rules of Engagement. There was insufficient time to create a target validation system in Cambodia similar to the large system allowing the American Embassy in Laos to validate targets. COMUSMACV, therefore, took the position that successful and timely initiation and continuance of the operation necessitated a military validation system among the FANK, JGS/RVNAF, and MACV. These representatives met in Saigon on 29 May 1970, at which time a Memorandum of Agreement on Rules of Engagement in Cambodia was signed.[14/]

FACs would control all airstrikes, except those validated and cleared for delivery by radar. Pilots were authorized to return ground fire immediately unless it came from an urban area, town, village, or hamlet; in these instances FANK validation of the target was required. If ground fire were not received, airstrikes against populated areas required the known presence of enemy forces or storage areas plus FANK validation of the target. If noncombatants were present, the strike was not to be conducted until the inhabitants had been warned by loudspeakers or leaflets to leave the area. Strikes were prohibited on 15 areas of cultural value to the Cambodian people, unless the target were requested and validated by FANK.

The ROE provided for the FANK to designate special operating areas in which there were no friendly forces, noncombatants, or populace. Prior approval was granted by the FANK to strike any target in these areas suspected to contain enemy forces, supplies, or installations. To prevent injury to the populace who might use or live along the waterways and overland routes traveled by the enemy, those certified for airstrikes were to be identified as Category A or B LOCs. Category A LOCs were those along which there were no friendly personnel, traffic, installations, or dwellings.

# INTERDICTION TARGET REQUEST NET

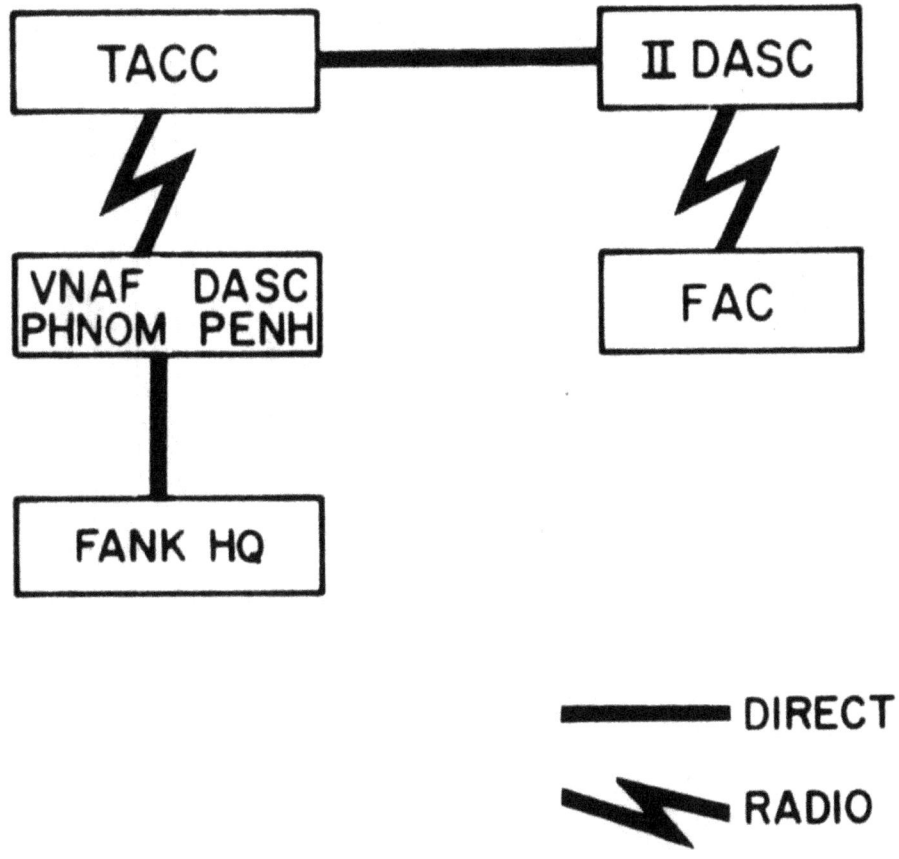

FIGURE 38

Airstrikes within 1,000 meters of each side of the waterway or route were permitted against any suspected targets. Category B LOCs were those used by the enemy but along which there were friendly personnel, traffic, installations, or dwellings. Prior to initial airstrikes along Category B LOCs, psychological warfare aircraft had to drop leaflets or use loudspeakers to warn the populace not to travel at night and that during daylight hours any motor-powered boat or motor vehicle observed would be destroyed. After such warning, aircraft were allowed to strike any motor vehicle or moving watercraft at night and all motor-powered boats or vehicles during daylight hours. Category B strikes were restricted to 500 meters on each side of the LOC and to within 500 meters of any inhabited village or hamlet containing 15 or more structures. A LOC could contain both Category A and B segments divided by distinguishing geographic points.

The communications net for requesting and validating targets is depicted in Fig. 38. The initial link between Phnom Penh and 7AF was one 100 word-per-minute TWX with very circuitous routing. The situation was somewhat alleviated with the establishment of radio communications between the VNAF DASC at Phnom Penh and 7AF TACC in early June. All communications from the FANK were routed through the VNAF DASC to the TACC which in turn controlled the FAC and fighter aircraft through II DASC. Two English-speaking FANK liaison officers were located at 7AF TACC with authority to validate targets for immediate strike request from FACs operating without an on-board FANK observer. They maintained current intelligence of the location of friendly forces and noncombatants in the interdiction area and passed this information to the FANK observers at Pleiku. Three English-speaking FANK aerial observers flew with the FACs out of Pleiku. They too had authority to declare a potential target hostile or friendly, so that immediate airstrikes could be directed against fleeting targets.

The ROE provided for use of ARC LIGHT strikes in special operating areas and along Category A LOCs. All other ARC LIGHT targets required validation by the senior FANK liaison officer at the TACC. The implanting of IGLOO WHITE seismic and acoustic sensors was permitted anywhere in the interdiction area, and area-denial weapons could be used in special operating areas, along Category A LOCs, and in any other area validated for such munitions by the senior FANK liaison officer.[15/]

The signing of Rules of Engagement on 29 May 1970 completed planning for the operation.

## Target Development

The initial assumption behind the establishment of an interdiction area in Cambodia was that there was a well-developed LOC system which could be interdicted in much the same way that operations in STEEL TIGER had been conducted during the previous several years. If this were the case, it was reasoned, then a mission of surveillance and attack would be appropriate. Information on Cambodia was scarce, however.[16/] Although 7AF had been working on building a Cambodian target base since the beginning of operations in May, there had been little information on possible LOC status or targets beyond the 30-kilometer limit of American penetration.[17/]

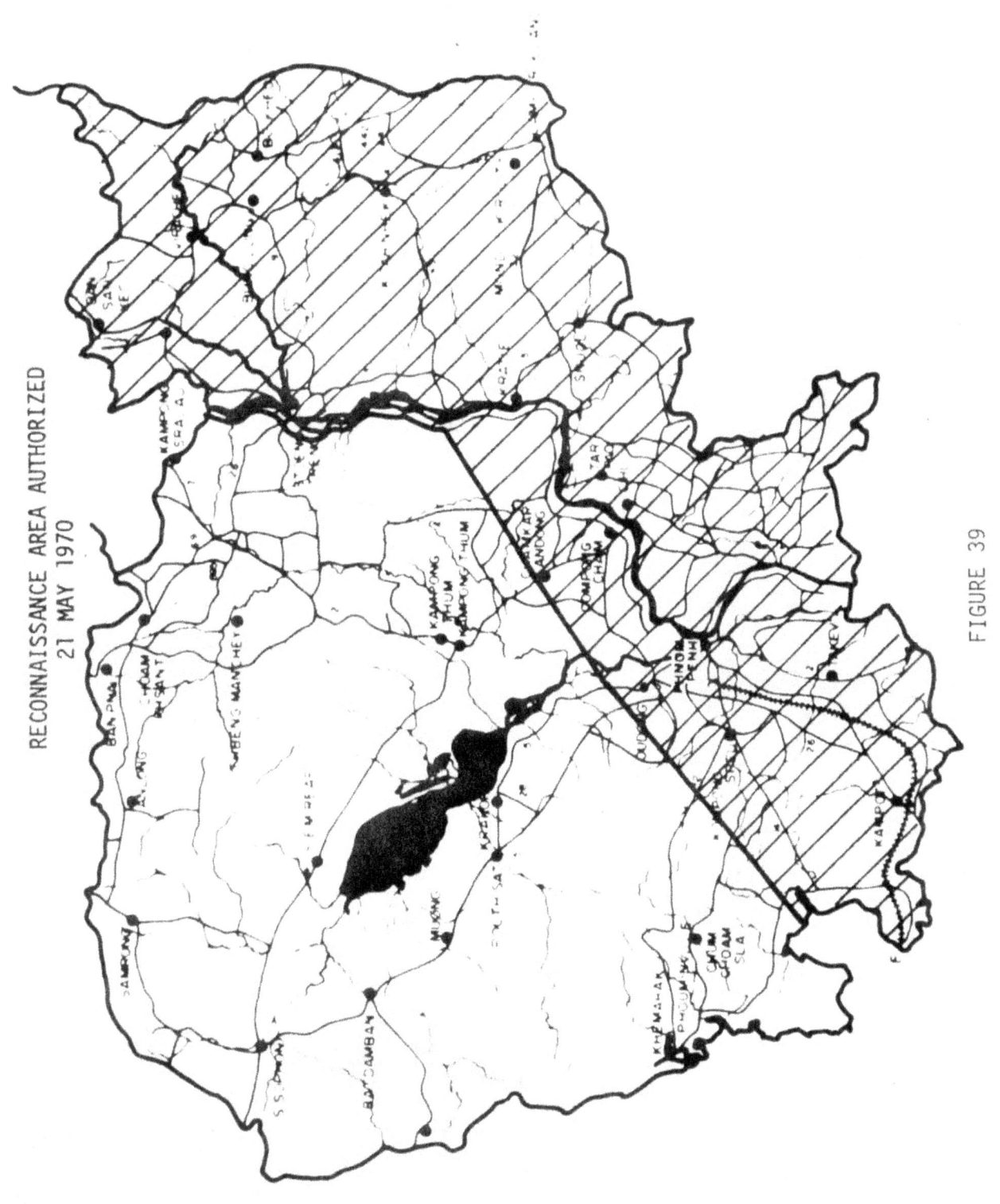

FIGURE 39

FIGURE 4Q

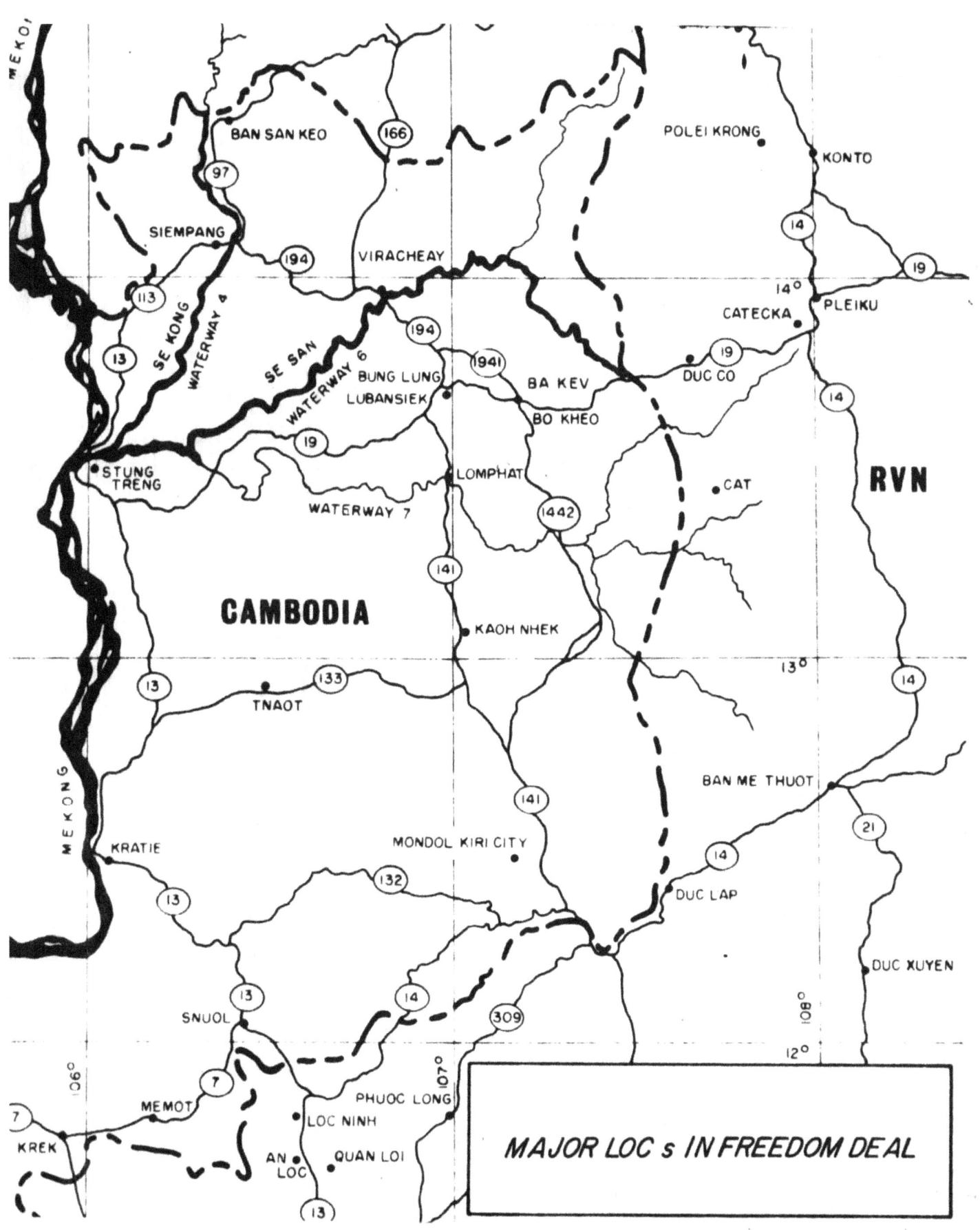
FIGURE 41

On 20 May, the JCS requested submission of a list of targets in Cambodia for interdiction operations.[18/] By that date, the target development process for Cambodia, initially applied within the 30-kilometer area, had been expanded to include the Northeast, but no targets had yet been identified. Seventh Air Force intelligence personnel narrowed some 3,640 inputs to the target data base down to a possible 52 targets suitable for interdiction. Personnel from the TACC, with experience as fast-mover FACs, reviewed existing maps and photography of the Cambodian LOC network and picked 25 possible targets. The results of the two efforts were merged, and a consolidated list of 25 targets was dispatched to the JCS on 21 May by MACV.[19/] These targets included 18 fords, bridges, and interdiction points (IDPs); three POL storage areas; one general storage area; one military complex; one strong point; and one fort complex.[20/] It was generally agreed, however, that more photo, infrared (IR), ARDF, and visual reconnaissance was needed to produce a really satisfactory list of possible targets.[21/]

Systematic surveillance of Cambodian LOCs had begun on 1 May 1970 and visual reconnaissance over other Cambodian areas on 9 May.[22/] On 21 May, CINCPAC expanded the reconnaissance area by authorizing flights over Cambodia in an area bounded on the east by the RVN Border, on the north by the Laotian Border, on the west by a line one kilometer west of the Mekong River to its intersection with a line 60 kilometers from the RVN Border, thence south along the 60 kilometer line to the Gulf of Thailand (Fig. 39). Flights in the vicinity of Phnom Penh were prohibited.[23/] The

45

reconnaissance program was further broadened on 22 May when the JCS authorized a one-time GIANT NAIL (U-2) overflight of 43 airfields throughout Cambodia.[24]

Absorption of the Cambodian workload by existing reconnaissance assets was done primarily by decreasing the number of sorties flown in RVN, although some increase in total sorties was also necessary. The average number of reconnaissance sorties flown in RVN per day during April was 22. This number dropped to 16 on 3 May, 10 on 6 May, and 8 on 8 May, while the number flown in Cambodia during the first 8 days of May rose from 0 on 1 May to 7 on 3 May, and 17 by 8 May. For the month, the average was 14 per day in RVN, 11 per day in Cambodia, and 2 per day that covered targets in RVN and Cambodia. The daily average of in-country reconnaissance sorties thus increased from 22 in April to 27 in May.

On 31 May, management of Cambodian reconnaissance was shifted to the out-country reconnaissance branch of Headquarters 7AF. This caused the number of reconnaissance sorties designated as out-country and flown by RVN based aircraft to increase from a daily average of 12 in May to a daily average of 18 in June. This increased sortie rate was met by assets previously flown for in-country missions. The Cambodian mission had no significant impact on the number of sorties flown in Laos since that number decreased in May due to poor weather. On 28 June, the reconnaissance force over Cambodia was augmented by two aircraft from Udorn RTAFB.[25]

EC-47 aircraft flew airborne radio direction finding orbits along

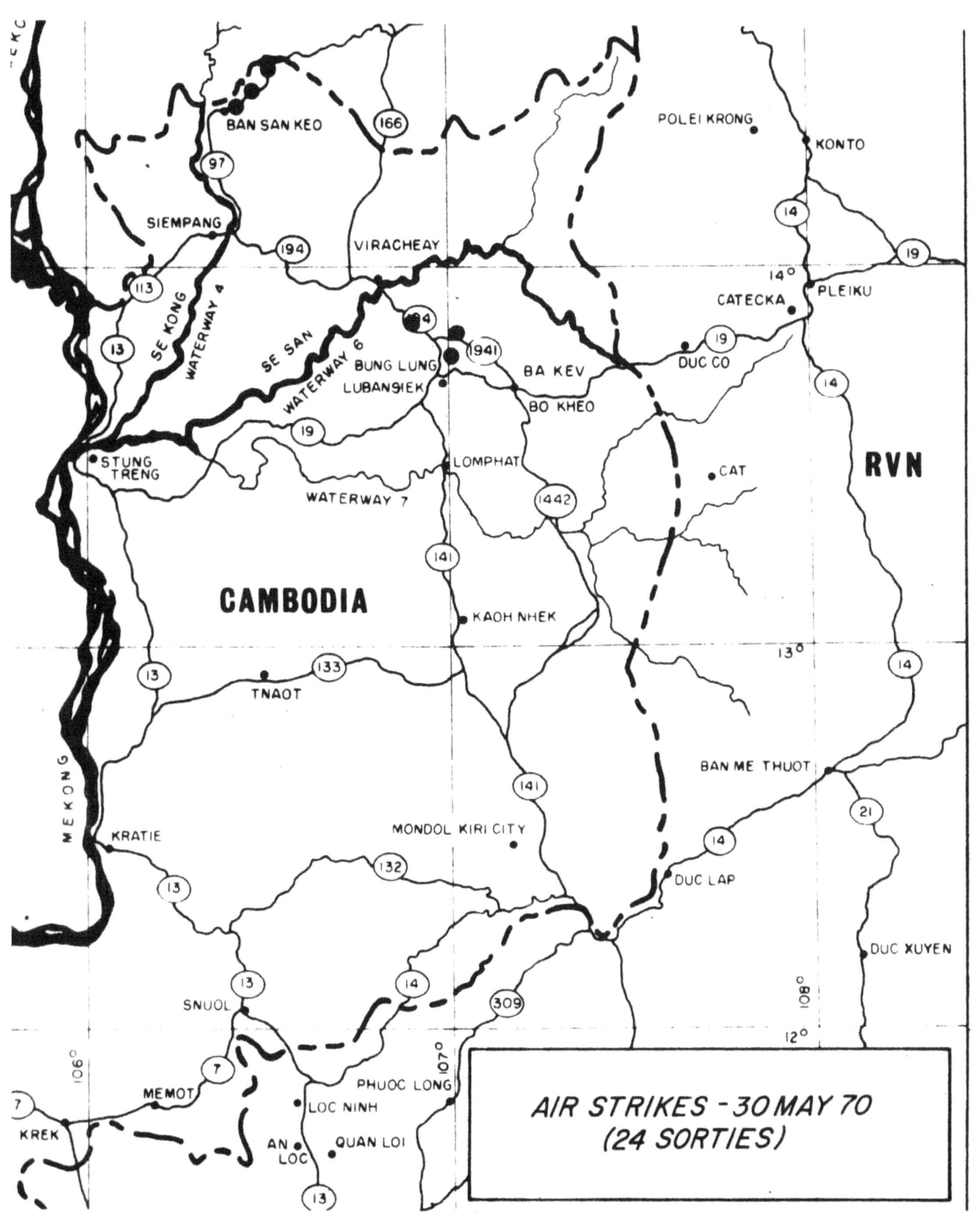

FIGURE 42

the Cambodian/RVN Border. This activity was extended into the Lomphat area on 7 May; and on 26 May, ARDF missions were authorized for the entire northeast area, adding still another source of targeting information.[26]

At the 29 May meeting, FANK officers validated for immediate strike three fords, three IDPs, and two bridges from the original list of 25 sent to the JCS.[27] Six of these targets were struck the following day by 24 fighter sorties (Fig. 42). Three of the targets were a bridge and two fords on Route 97, the only route leading from Attopeu, in southern Laos, into Cambodia. The other three were a ford and two IDPs on roads leading into the area of Lomphat, Bakiev, and Labansiek. Of the two not struck, one was a bridge found to already have one span down and the other an IDP found to be within 500 meters of a village.[28]

By 1 June 1970, targeting was rapidly falling into the mold that had been successfully built by experience in Laos. VR, photo reconnaissance, and other intelligence sources were being used to develop a computerized targeting list containing all pertinent information available on any particular target. In addition, previous strikes on the target and BDA were recorded. Since the interdiction effort was still relatively small, the object was to build a "shopping list" for the FANK in its search for lucrative targets, and to increase the capability for more extensive operations if they were needed.[29]

## Operation FREEDOM DEAL

The 24 strikes on 30 May marked the beginning of interdiction beyond the 30-kilometer limit originally established for U.S. operations in Cambodia. There were no further interdiction strikes until 4 June when, after extensive leaflet drops and loudspeaker warnings to the populace, 34 sorties struck 11 targets (Fig. 43). These strikes destroyed or damaged 10 watercraft, 40 structures, 9 bulldozers and roadgraders, started 8 secondary fires, and destroyed numerous POL drums.[30/] Interdiction strikes were flown daily after 4 June. The interdiction operation was christened FREEDOM DEAL by CINCPAC on 6 June with the publication of the FREEDOM DEAL Basic Operations Order. The mission was: "To maintain surveillance of enemy activities in Cambodia, east of the Mekong River...and to attack those activities as necessary to protect U.S. forces in the Republic of Vietnam." The tasks to be accomplished included: (1) destruction of those facilities and materials that contributed to the support of aggression and insurgencies in RVN; (2) interdiction, harassment, disruption, and impedance of movement of the enemy and his materials through Cambodia into the RVN; and (3) denial to the enemy of the use of LOCs in eastern Cambodia to the maximum extent possible.[31/]

The additional targets struck on 4 June had been validated by the FANK representatives when they returned to RVN on 2 June. They had actually come back with a rather permissive attitude toward interdiction and with a very large area validated for strikes at will. Acting on 7AF advice, however, they considerably reduced the special operating area and FANk

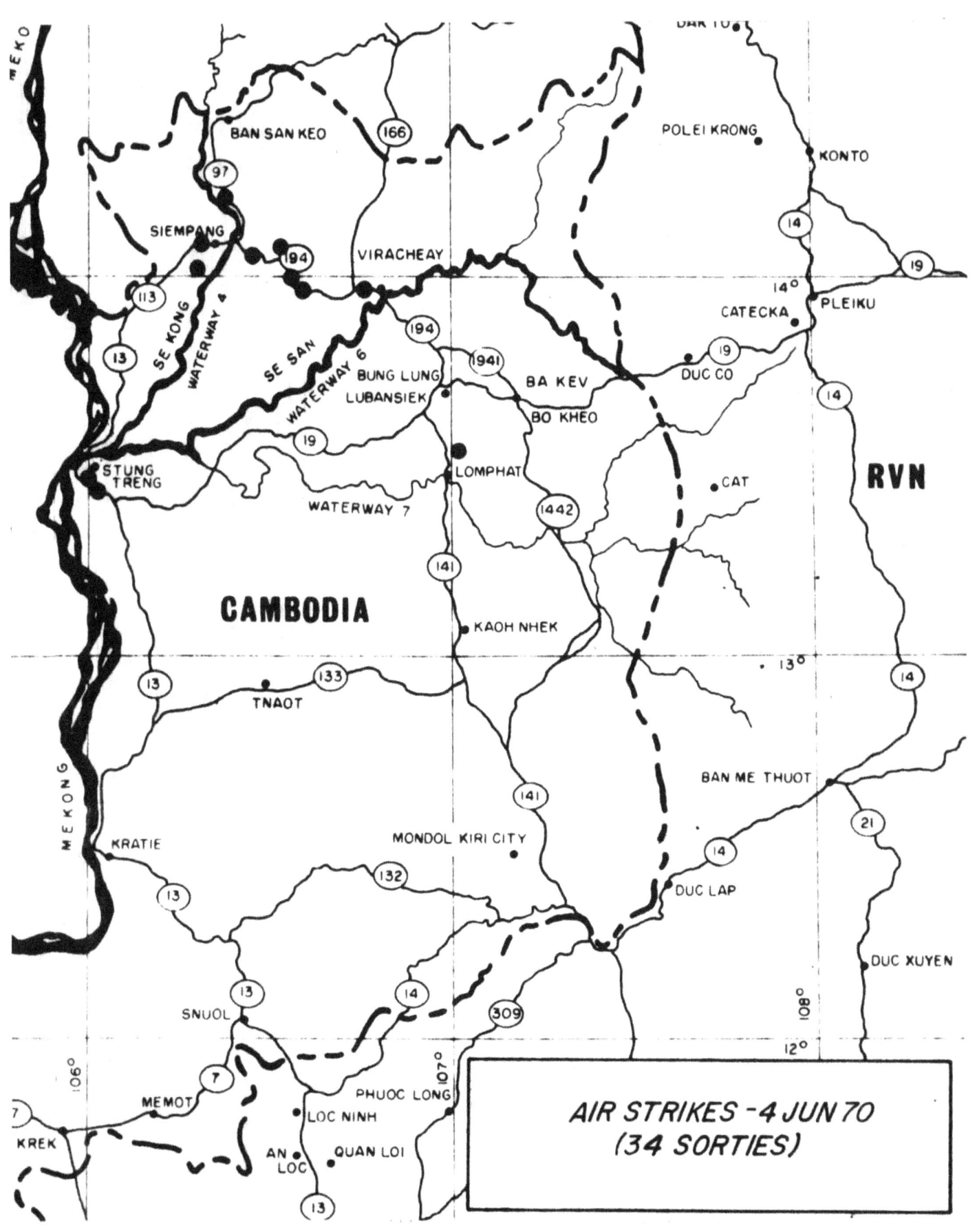

FIGURE 43

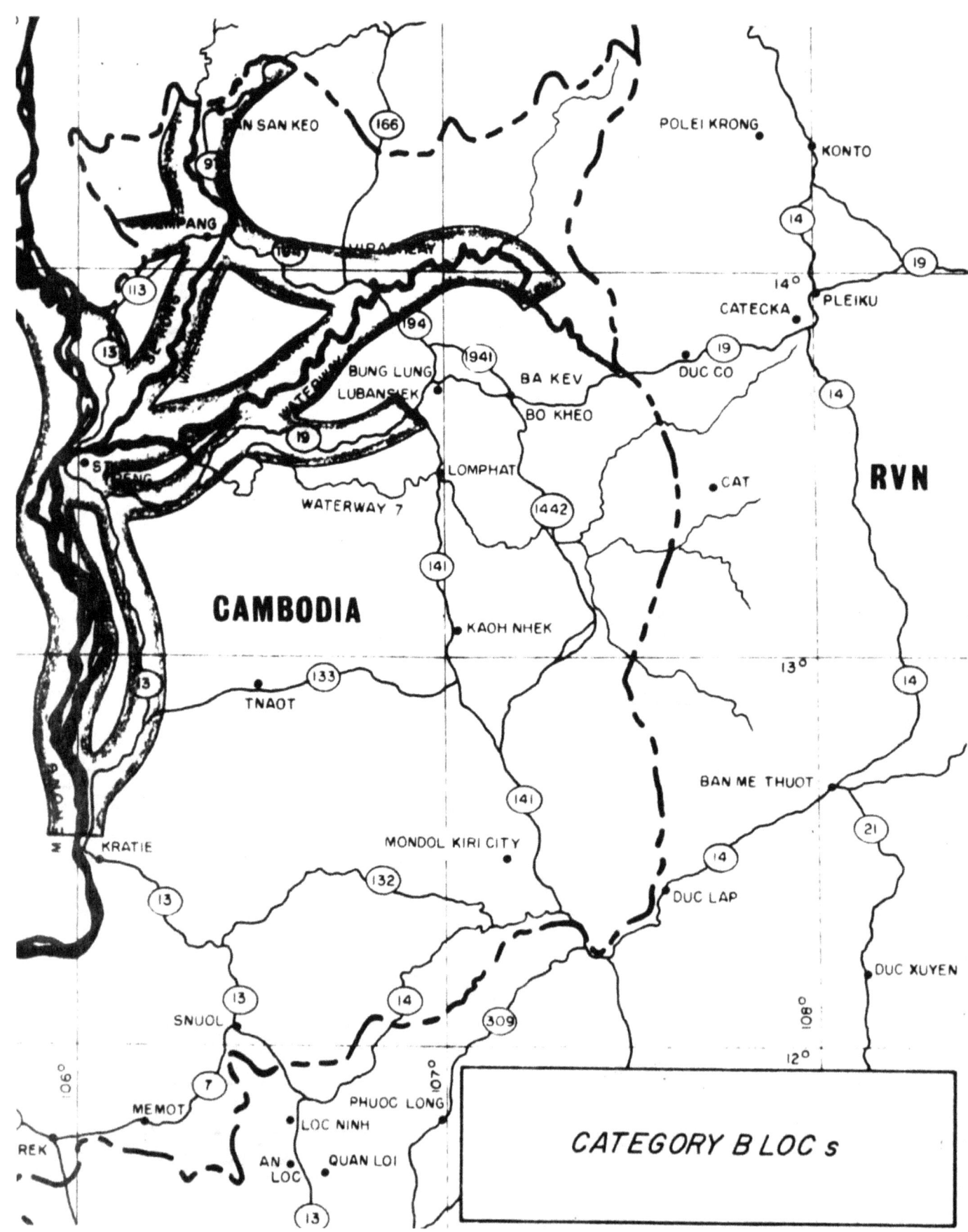

FIGURE 44

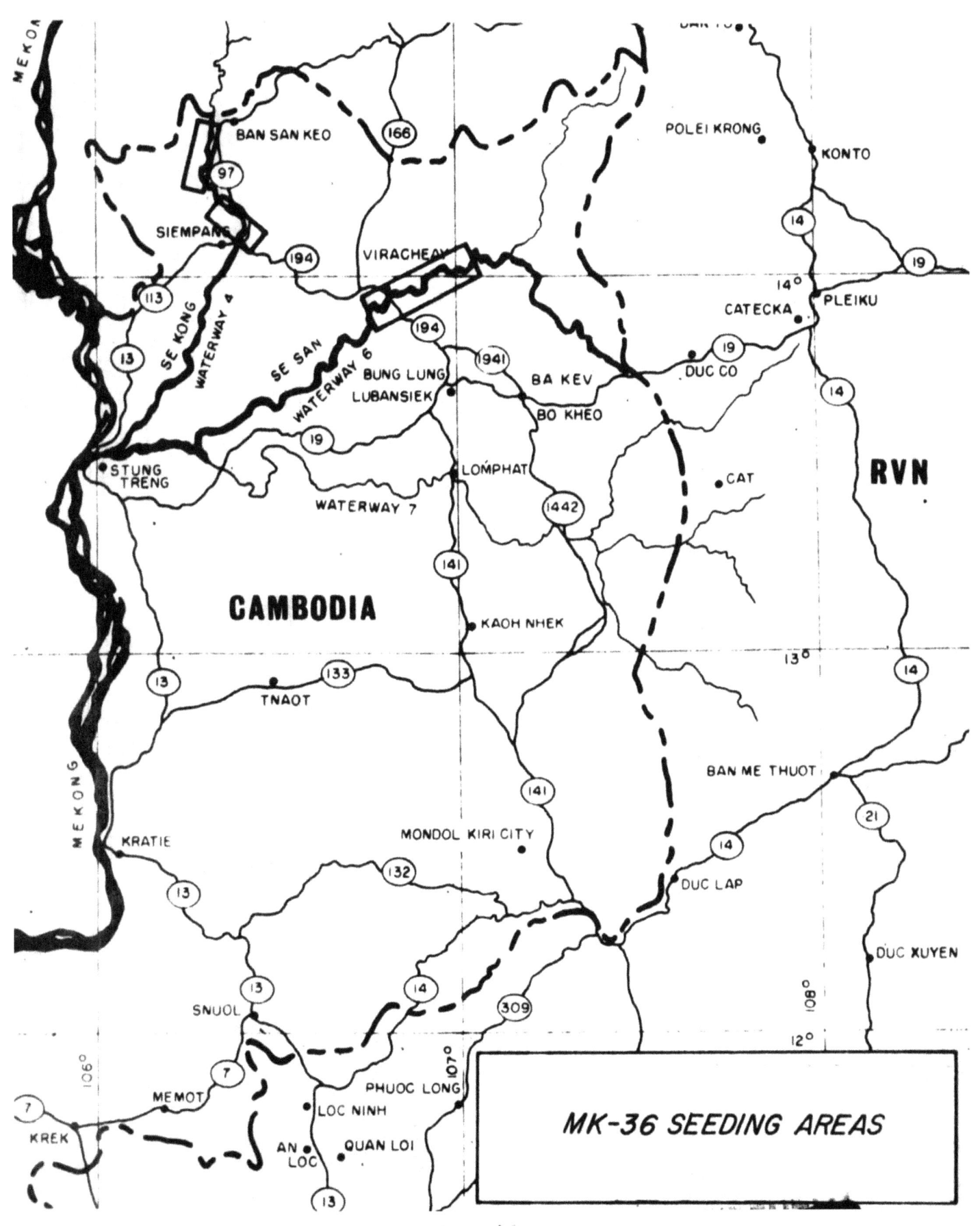

FIGURE 45

representatives became more cautious in validating targets.[32/] On 4 June, five Cambodian Air Force officers were posted to RVN stations. Two were located at the TACC at Tan Son Nhut to validate targets, while the other three were placed at Pleiku to fly with the FACs to acquire and validate targets. After 9 June, only the FANK officers at the TACC could validate targets. The three flying with the FACs were limited to target nomination.[33/]

As provided in the ROE, a number of LOCs were designated as Category B. Those identified included portions of the Se Kong, Se San, and Mekong Rivers, Highway 13 from Kratie north to the Laos Border, and portions of Highways 194, 19, and 136 (Fig. 44).[34/] On 11 June, the entire Mekong River from Kratie to the Laos Border was validated as the Category B LOC.[35/]

By 15 June, more than 550 MK-36 mines had been placed in the Se Kong to inhibit water traffic into Cambodia from the Attopeu area of southern Laos. Mining was also carried out on the Se San to curtail supply shipment from the base areas in the northeast to the Mekong and on into the more populated areas of central Cambodia (Fig. 45).[36/]

Increased air surveillance was initiated in southern Laos, particularly the area of Attopeu and southward, to determine the quantity of supplies being shipped into Cambodia from that area. The NVA had captured Attopeu on 29 April. They also made a concerted effort to gain control of the LOCs along the eastern edge of the Bolovens Plateau. These efforts were viewed by 7AF Intelligence as possible forerunners of an increased supply corridor development into Cambodia. In early May, photo coverage of the waterways and roads in the vicinity of Attopeu was increased to twice a week, and the number of IGLOO WHITE sensor strings in the area increased from one to four. Visual reconnaissance of the entire area increased to monitor truck movements and, after the use of Thai-based resources in Cambodia was authorized on 3 June 1970, an AC-123 patrolled the area in southern Laos and into Cambodia on a nightly basis. There was very little river or vehicular traffic observed.[37/] On 8 June, COMUSMACV requested authority from the JCS to expand the tactical reconnaissance area to include all of Cambodia on a recurring basis.[38/] This authority was granted on 9 June with the restriction that flights would not be conducted in the vicinity of Phnom Penh, that those outside the interdiction area would be unarmed, and that flak suppression would not be employed.[39/] To cover the expanded area, tactical reconnaissance missions increased from 315 sorties in May to 324 sorties during the first 20 days in June with 424 reconnaissance objectives completed.[40/]

Both preplanned and immediate attack sorties were allocated to the interdiction campaign. During the period 1-20 June, prior to expansion of the interdiction area, 414 preplanned and 224 immediate sorties were flown into the FREEDOM DEAL area (Fig. 46). About 320 were flown by F-4s, 246 by F-100s, 50 by A-37s, and 12 by A-1s.[41/] All but 21 of the strikes came from in-country resources. Cumulative BDA for FREEDOM DEAL through 20 June included 94 vehicles, 112 watercraft, 446 military structures, and five bridges destroyed or damaged.[42/] The area of concentration of the initial interdiction strikes was the LOCs from Stung Treng north to

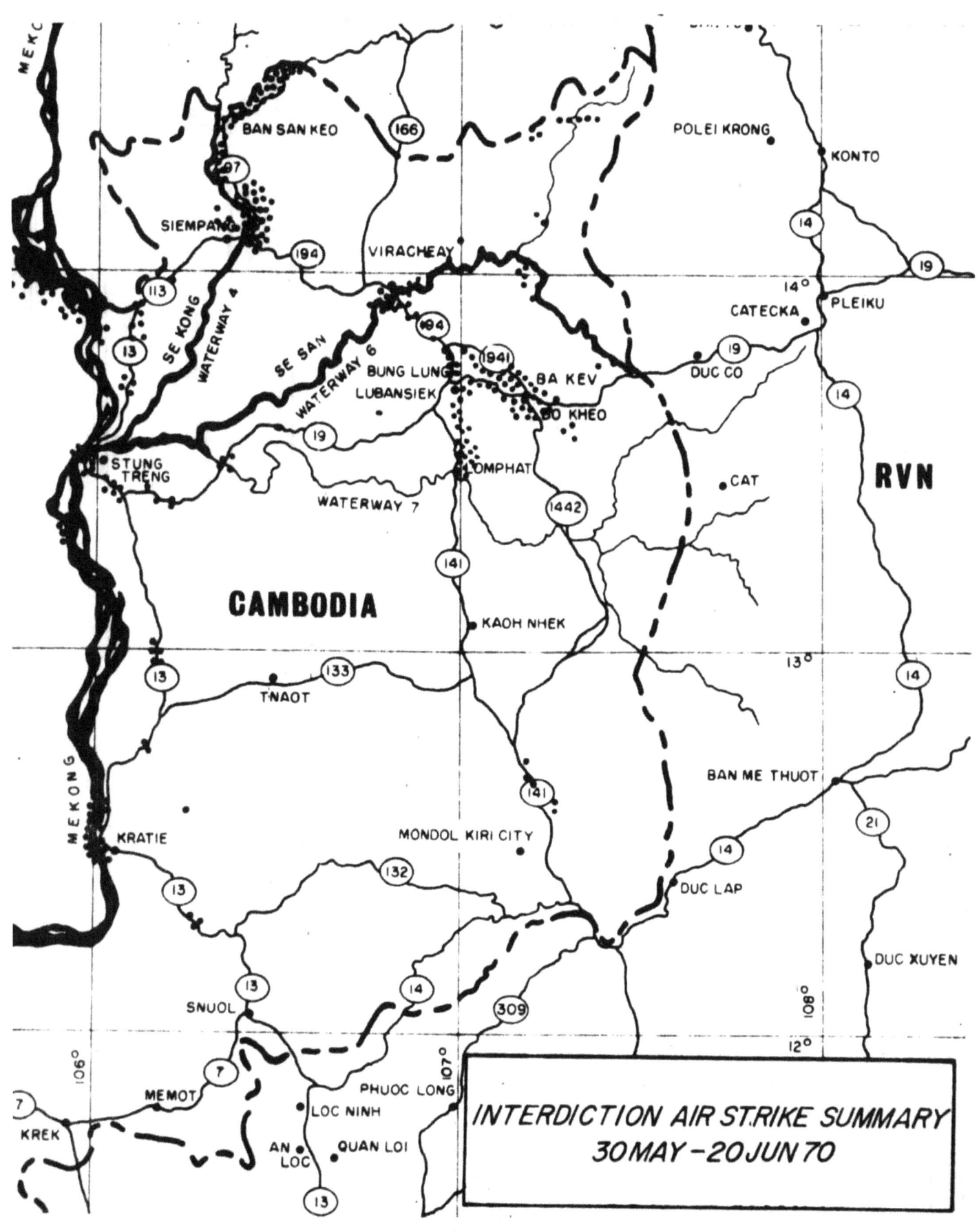

FIGURE 46

the Laos Border. On 7 June, additional sorties were allocated into the Lomphat, Labansiek, Bakiev triangle. A fairly even distribution between the two areas was evident until 13 June when the Lomphat, Labansiek, Bakiev region became the primary interdiction area. This general pattern of sortie allocation continued until 20 June.[43/]

The initial thrust of FREEDOM DEAL was interdiction, but it became obvious by the end of the second week in June that some air support for Cambodian ground units was vital. This became graphically clear in the case of Labansiek and Bakiev, the last holdouts of the FANK in the northeast. The VNAF had participated in the evacuation of Lomphat on 31 May, but by 20 June, U.S. aircraft had performed interdiction only in the FREEDOM DEAL area.

During the first week in June, the enemy attacked Labansiek on numerous occasions. He also increased his activity around Bakiev. As the heavy ground action continued after 13 June, USAF personnel applied interdiction in its broadest sense and fighters began attacking known enemy locations around Labansiek and Bakiev under FAC or COMBAT SKYSPOT control. Gunships also attacked enemy units threatening the towns; the gunships served as their own FACs, operating visually and with the assistance of a radar beacon installed at Bakiev. Because of troop losses and supply and reinforcement problems, the Cambodian government decided to evacuate the two northeastern strongholds. The evacuation began on 23 June under continuous USAF fighter cover. The primary evacuation aircraft were USAF C-123s and C-7s. An ARVN relief column also arrived at

Labansiek on 23 June and by 1830H on the 26th, the last of more than 7,000 refugees had exited into RVN. The government withdrawal from northeast Cambodia left that entire area essentially under control of the enemy.[44/]

Expanded Interdiction

On 15 June 1970, 7AF asked COMUSMACV to broaden the area of air operations and to interpret the interdiction function more broadly. 7AF stressed how limited the enemy logistic activity was along the LOCs in Cambodia, as compared to the situation in Laos, and suggested that U.S. air be used primarily for close air support and secondarily for interdiction. The 7AF plan involved the incorporation of U.S. and VNAF forces with FANK personnel in the control network, including TACPs and the DASC at Phnom Penh. It also envisioned an increased FAC/VR reconnaissance and intelligence effort. This anticipated increase in operations was to be absorbed by current 7AF resources without seriously curtailing existing operations.[45/]

The following day COMUSMACV received a message from the Chairman, Joint Chiefs of Staff (CJCS) stressing the need to broaden the interpretation of interdiction in Cambodia. Reporting on a meeting with President Nixon, Admiral Moorer, Acting CJCS, pointed out that the President had stressed the need to expand intelligence gathering, to be more effective in employment of air, and to apply a broad interpretation of the term interdiction, especially after U.S. troop withdrawals from Cambodia on 30 June.[46/] On 17 June, a message from the JCS broadened the entire interdiction concept and established the basis for expanded interdiction in

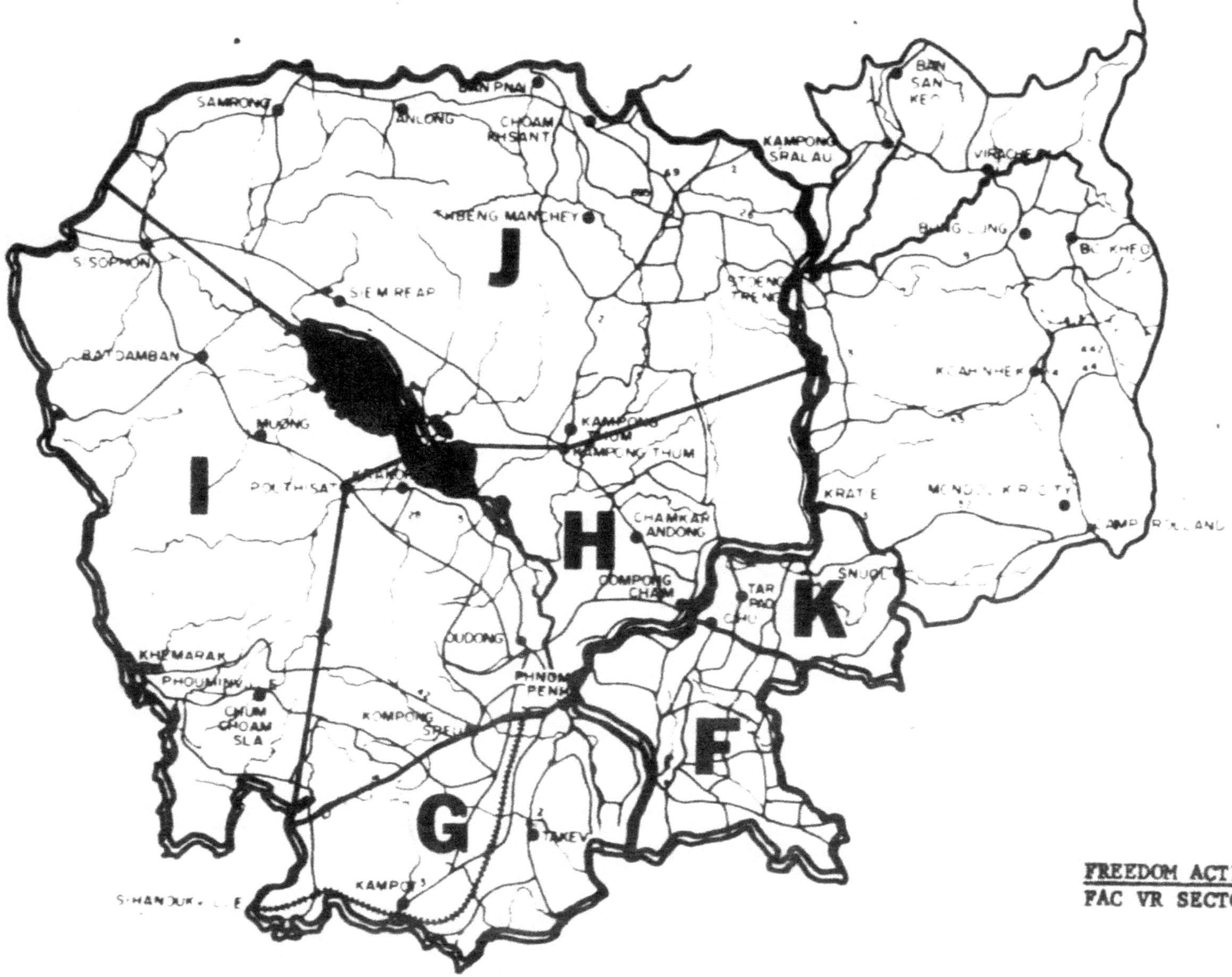

**FREEDOM ACTION**
**FAC VR SECTORS**

FIGURE 47

what became known as Operation FREEDOM ACTION. With respect to the increased use of air, the message said, "...you are authorized to employ U.S. tactical air interdiction in any situation which involves a serious threat to major Cambodian positions such as a provincial capital whose loss would constitute a serious military or psychological blow to the coungry."[47/]

On 18 June, COMUSMACV officially requested the interdiction area be expanded to include that part of Cambodia bounded by a line 200 meters west of the Mekong River on the west and Route 7 on the south (this eventually became the FREEDOM DEAL extension shown in Fig. 35). He further requested standby authority until 31 September 1970 to conduct tactical air interdiction and B-52 strikes outside the interdiction area on a casy-by-case basis. The proposed strikes would exclude the area within 20 kilometers of Phnom Penh, national monuments and shrines, and areas of cultural value to the Cambodian people. All targets would be validated by the FANK.[48/] CINCPAC interpreted the JCS message of 17 June as authorization to employ U.S. tactical air beyond the current limits of the Cambodian interdiction area and communicated this to COMUSMACV on 19 June.[49/] In this way, the JCS message of 17 June became the justification for an expanded interdiction campaign that became FREEDOM ACTION.

As an initial step in implementation of FREEDOM ACTION, the TACC established six FAC/VR sectors, designated F through K, in that portion of Cambodia not covered by FREEDOM DEAL (Fig. 47). Four OV-10s from Ubon RTAFB, Thailand, covered sector Juliet beginning on 20 June and four

OV-10s from Utapao RTAFB began coverage of sector India on 21 June; these sorties were subtracted from the STEEL TIGER allocations.[50/] Sectors Foxtrot, Golf, Hotel, and Kilo were covered by 16 aircraft from the resources of III DASC in RVN beginning on 23 June. Foxtrot was handled by O-1s from Tay Ninh East, Golf by O-1s and O-2s from Chau Doc, Hotel by OV-10s from Bien Hoa, and Kilo by O-2s and OV-10s from Tay Ninh. Stormy F-4s also operated in all areas of Cambodia as needed. FACs dedicated to the Cambodian operation flew all FAC missions there. In addition to VR of major LOCs and photography of route structures and other possible target areas, the FACs closely monitored major cities and provincial capitals for signs of enemy activity. As possible targets were located, identified, and photographed, they were reported to 7AF TACC for validation by FANK officers.[51/]

The primary air request channel to 7AF TACC was through the VNAF DASC at Phnom Penh, call sign Toulouse, which by 20 June had HF, UHF, and FM frequencies available. Backup communications for immediate airstrikes in sectors F, G, H, and K could be transmitted through III DASC to the TACC. FAC requests for immediates in sectors I and J went directly through III DASC (Fig. 48).[52/] Flight following was provided by the Paris Combat Reporting Center at Tan Son Nhut.

It was initially believed sufficient French-speaking VNAF FACs qualified to direct U.S. strikes would be available to operate in sectors F, G, H, and K, so that communications with the Cambodians would not present a problem.[53/] Fewer were available than anticipated, however,

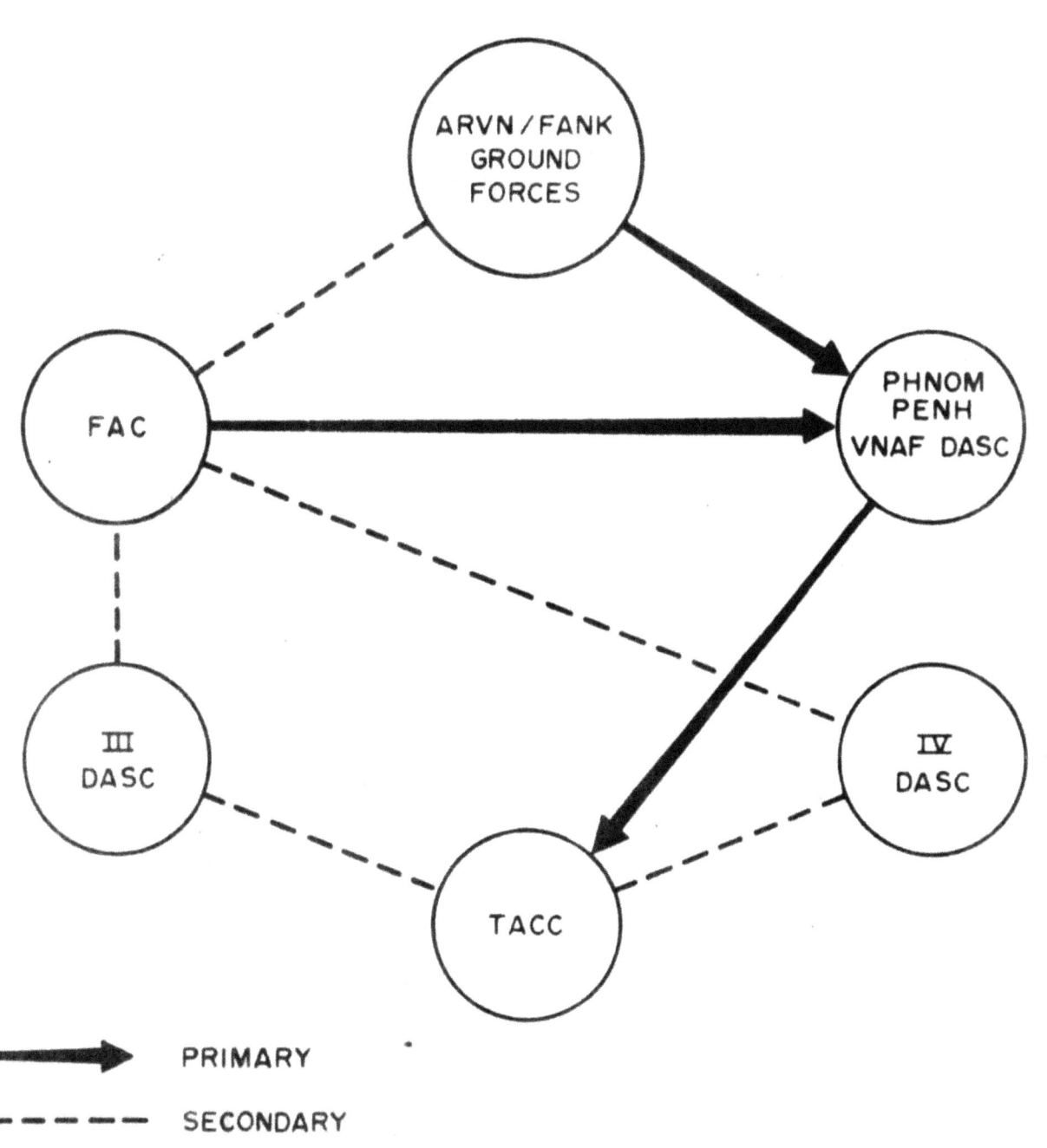

FIGURE 48

and there were also few FANK Liaison Officers who could speak English. As a result, it became necessary to use USAF officers and airmen who were fluent in French to act as airborne interpreters. Although 7AF was able to fill this need from SEA resources, none of the officers was on flying status and none had attended the appropriate survival schools; thus waivers had to be obtained to employ them.[54/]

Procedures also had to be established for communication between USAF FACs, VNAF FACs, and Cambodian Air Force aircraft. This was facilitated by establishing three common frequencies for establishing initial contact by radio. A common frequency was also established for initial contact between ground personnel and FACs. Since a majority of the FANK Liaison Officers had never worked with any type of air support previously, an instruction sheet was prepared by the TACC on how to use airplanes for air support, how to signal them, and related items. Provisions were also established for a proposed communications network incorporating an Airborne Battlefield Command and Control Center (ABCCC).[55/] The ABCCC concept had not been implemented as of 1 July.

The Rules of Engagement for FREEDOM ACTION were the same as those for FREEDOM DEAL. There were no Category B LOCs, however, and targets identified by the ground commanders were considered validated.[56/]

USAF aircraft flew their first strikes in the FREEDOM ACTION area on 20 June. On that date, 16 sorties struck enemy positions in the vicinity of Kampong Thom.[57/] That city had been under enemy pressure since

4 June, when a force of at least regimental size attacked the city. Although the city had been reinforced, fighting continued in the vicinity for the next week. As the month progressed, the situation became more tenuous. On 15-16 June, VNAF helicopters airlifted additional Cambodian troops to Kampong Thom as enemy forces moved within .7 kilometers of the center of the city. By 20 June, it was feared the city might fall at any time,[58/] and on that date MACV directed 7AF to provide air support for the defenders. Two AC-119G gunship sorties, two UC-123K flareship sorties, and six fighter sorties supported friendly positions on 20 June. Through 22 June, approximately 12 gunship and 46 tactical air sorties flew in support of the town and by the end of the month, 82 fighter sorties had struck enemy positions in the vicinity.[59/]

Airstrikes also supported the defense of Siem Reap, a key point on Route 6 in the Northwest, the site of Cambodia's only international airport outside of Phnom Penh, and the gateway city to Angkor Wat. Siem Reap was unsuccessfully attacked by Khmer Rouge forces on 8 and 10 June, and by the middle of the month the enemy occupied Angkor Wat. The Lon Nol government expressed fear that enemy occupation of the ruins at Angkor Wat would lead to the establishment of Prince Sihanouk there as head of a government in exile, and that this would further undermine the popular strength of the present government. Although Siem Reap was not threatened during the latter part of June, the airstrikes did aid the defenders in dislodging enemy units in outlying areas.[60/]

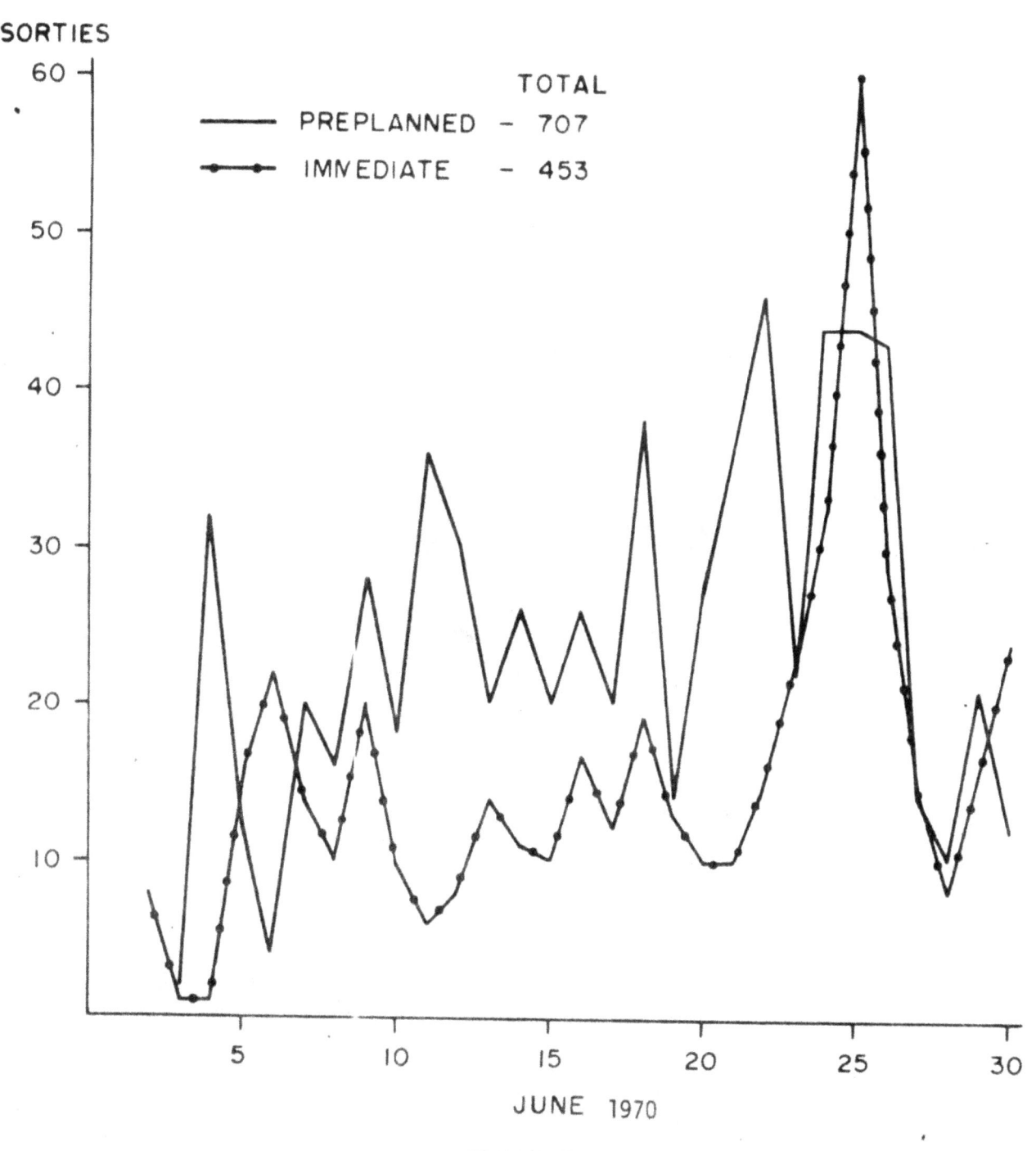

FIGURE 49

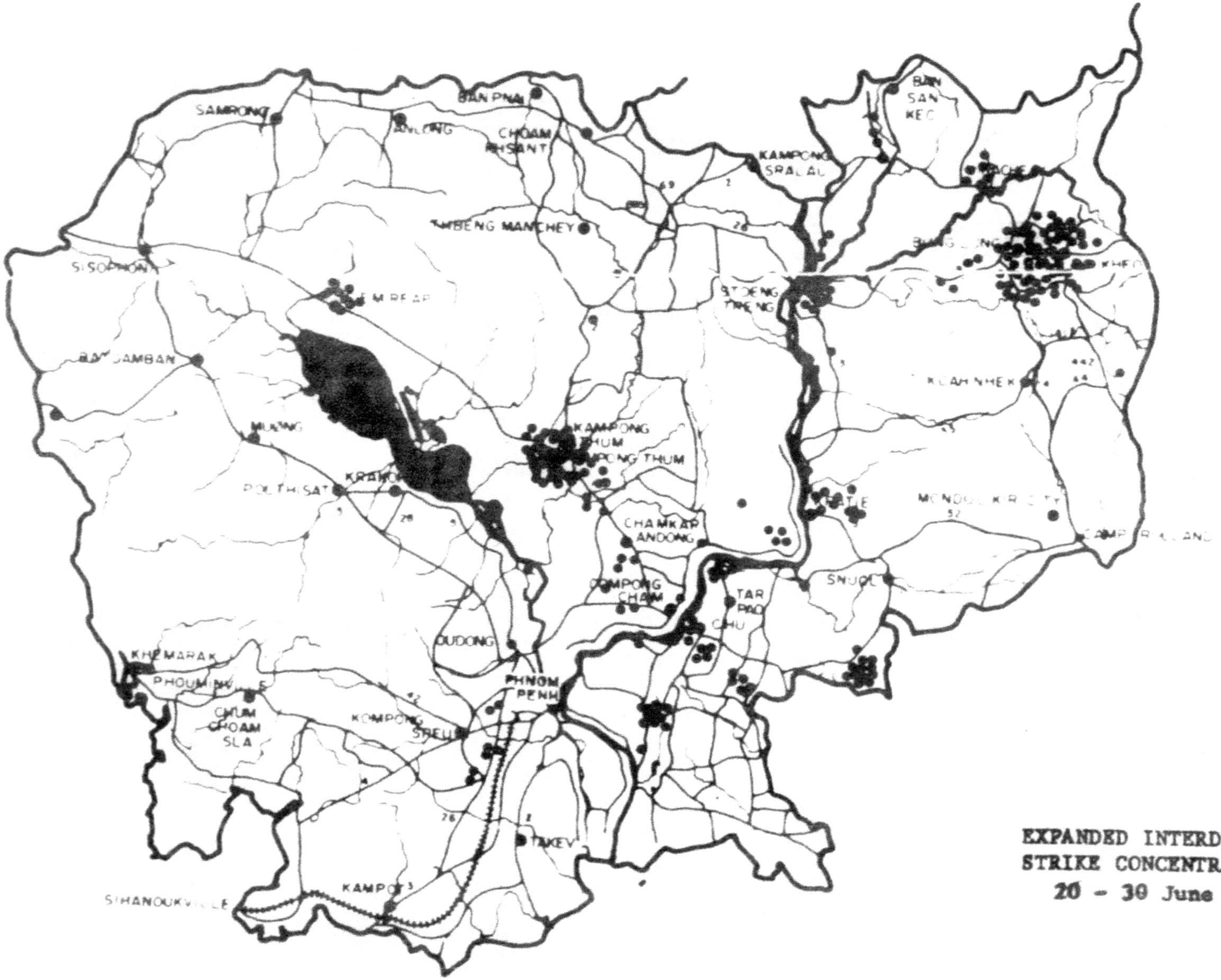

EXPANDED INTERDICTION
STRIKE CONCENTRATIONS
20 - 30 June 1970

FIGURE 50

During the ten days of the expanded interdiction campaign, 20-30 June 1970, some 226 sorties were flown in the expanded interdiction area, outside the limits of FREEDOM DEAL (Fig. 49). Targets included vehicles, key points on LOCs, enemy weapon positions, storage areas, and known enemy troop locations. During the ten-day period, however, most of the tactical airstrikes in Cambodia were in the FREEDOM DEAL area, still primarily concentrated around Lomphat, Labansiek, and Bakiev (Fig. 50).

The stress that had been placed on the protection of cultural, historic, and artistic properties throughout Cambodia was again emphasized as the expanded interdiction effort progressed. On 19 June 1970, a list of cultural sites was issued along with a restriction prohibiting strikes within 1,000 meters. Aircraft were to withdraw if ground fire were received from the restricted area. As photographs of each area were produced by 7AF reconnaissance units, prints were sent to all FACs, gunship units, tactical air units, and headquarters concerned with the Cambodian operation to aid them in identifying these historic areas. In addition, books of pictures of these cultural sites with maps showing their location were made up by the 12th Reconnaissance Intelligence Technical Squadron and sent to the commanders of major air units and DASCs in RVN. Copies were also sent to the Thai and Cambodian governments. As more sites were successfully identified and photographed, pictures were forwarded to the major units and the books were updated. The restricted list was further expanded by the FANK representatives on 28 June.[61/] The campaign requirement that all targets be validated by FANK representatives provided further safeguards.

57

From the outset of the interdiction campaign, the Typhoon A-37 FAC operation had been viewed as a temporary measure. On 26 June, the FAC/VR sectors throughout Cambodia were slightly realigned. Echo sector was eliminated and A, B, C, D, and K were expanded to cover that area (Fig. 51). [62/] On 28 June, the FAC/VR activity of the A-37s from Bien Hoa was discontinued. [63/]

On 29 June, COMUSMACV notified 7AF that the authority which had established the FREEDOM ACTION operation, JCS 172344Z June 1970, was not to be continued to indicate the establishment of a major interdiction campaign throughout Cambodia. All strikes outside the FREEDOM DEAL area, he pointed out, were to be approved by COMUSMACV on a case-by-case basis. [64/] This apparent change in direction for the campaign was further clarified by two messages on 30 June which set out the limits of operations effective 1 July. The interdiction area was restricted to the FREEDOM DEAL area, except that the eastern limits were extended to the RVN Border rather than to the 30-kilometer line as previously approved. In addition, a FREEDOM DEAL Extension was identified for selective tactical air and B-52 strikes. Its limits were Route 13 on the north, a line 200 meters west of the Mekong River on the west, the RVN Border on the east, and a line 200 meters south of Route 7 from 200 meters west of the Mekong River to the intersection with Route 78 and thence south-southwest along Route 78 to the RVN Border (Fig. 35). Operations in the extended area were to be against only identified, highly lucrative targets that posed a substantial threat to Allied forces. Further provisions allowed air reconnaissance over all of Cambodia but with armed escort and flak suppression permitted only in

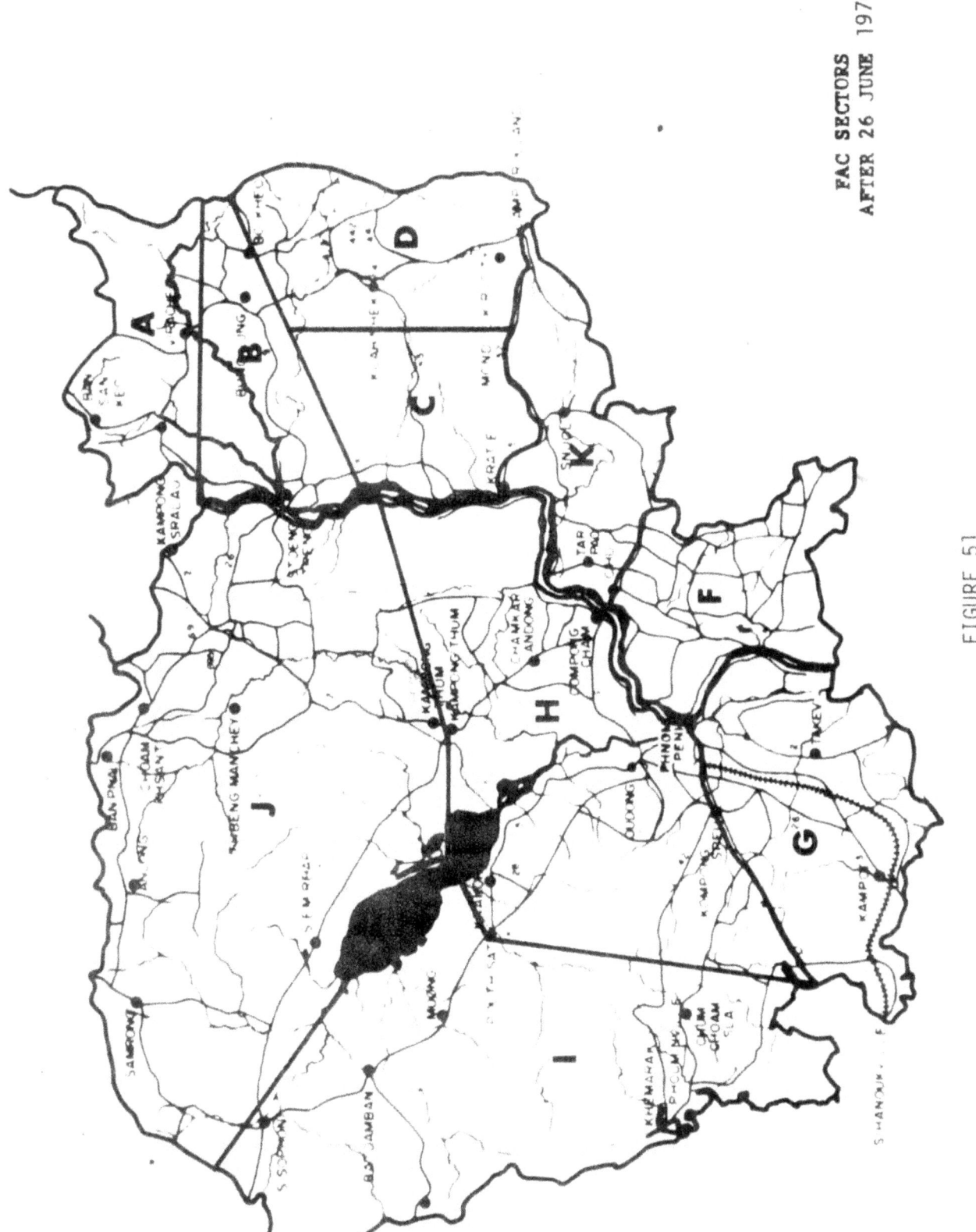

FAC SECTORS
AFTER 26 JUNE 1970

FIGURE 51

the original FREEDOM DEAL area. Search and rescue missions were allowed over all of Cambodia and were authorized to return ground fire received in the conduct of these operations.[65/]

By 1 July, 7AF, through Operation FREEDOM DEAL and the expanded interdiction operations associated with it, had succeeded in establishing an ongoing interdiction campaign in Cambodia. The number of LOCs interdicted would make enemy travel more difficult. Air support of beleaguered towns, such as Kampong Thom, had enabled them to survive the concerted enemy drive to take them. In addition, 7AF had established a target base with an ever-growing file of information on Cambodian targets and LOCs.

Operation FREEDOM DEAL presented the enemy with a much more difficult situation in Cambodia than would have been the case otherwise. Confronted with the need to resupply his forces almost entirely through Laos, the enemy now faced an interdiction force in being, ready to strike his resupply efforts at the first sign of activity. Any effort to expand his LOCs was also inhibited, since road construction equipment and any similar signs of activity in the interdiction area would prompt airstrikes upon detection and validation. The enemy was thus faced with having to anticipate running the gauntlet of U.S. interdiction from the entry points of his materiel into Laos from NVN, through the Laos panhandle, and throughout his LOC and storage areas in northeast Cambodia. Resupply would be a costly effort for the enemy.

# CHAPTER IV

## AIRLIFT SUPPORT

During the Cambodian campaign, the 834th Air Division provided the following airlift support within the borders of Cambodia: (1) between 23 May and 30 June, 169 C-7 sorties carried 245.8 tons of cargo and 328 passengers into O Rang Airfield; (2) on 23 and 24 June, 45 C-7 sorties and three C-123 sorties airlifted 3,130 refugees from Bung Lung and Ba Kiev Airfields in northeastern Cambodia to Pleiku, RVN; (3) on 29 and 30 June, eight C-130 sorties airlifted 110 tons of weapons and ammunition from Tan Son Nhut and Bien Hoa to Phnom Penh; (4) three C-130s airdropped 44 tons of ammunition to the 1st Air Cav Div at Firebase David near O Rang on 27 May; (5) a C-130 airdropped 4.4 tons of ammunition on 23 June and 5.6 tons of ammunition and radio gear on 29 June to Cambodian forces at Kampong Thom; (6) between 1 May and 27 June, C-130 aircraft delivered 20 COMMANDO VAULT weapons in dense jungle, clearing 16 helicopter landing zones. Figure 52 provides a statistical summary of airlift operations into 23 RVN airfields (Fig. 53) supporting operations in Cambodia between 28 April and 30 June 1967.

## TOTAL TONS (CARGO & PASSENGERS)

|  | 28-30 April | May | June | Total |
|---|---|---|---|---|
| C-7 | 455 | 4,042 | 3,512 | 8,009 |
| C-123 | 751 | 6,463 | 7,448 | 14,662 |
| C-130 | 1,411 | 23,990 | 18,544 | 43,945 |
| Total | 2,617 | 34,495 | 29,504 | 66,616 |
| All RVN Airlift | 9,116 | 110,344 | 98,065 | 217,525 |
| % of all RVN Airlift | 28.7% | 31.3% | 30.1% | 30.6% |

## CARGO TONS

|  | 28-30 April | May | June | Total |
|---|---|---|---|---|
| C-7 | 300 | 2,733 | 2,346 | 5,379 |
| C-123 | 466 | 4,860 | 5,534 | 10,860 |
| C-130 | 1,330 | 21,685 | 14,937 | 37,952 |
| Total | 2,096 | 29,278 | 22,817 | 54,191 |
| All RVN Airlift | 5,423 | 69,920 | 54,421 | 129,764 |
| % of all RVN Airlift | 38.7% | 41.9% | 41.9% | 41.8% |

## PASSENGERS

|  | 28-30 April | May | June | Total |
|---|---|---|---|---|
| C-7 | 1,174 | 10,907 | 9,710 | 21,791 |
| C-123 | 613 | 13,361 | 15,955 | 29,929 |
| C-130 | 678 | 19,204 | 30,060 | 49,942 |
| Total | 2,465 | 43,472 | 55,725 | 101,662 |
| All RVN Airlift | 30,779 | 336,868 | 363,698 | 731,345 |
| % of all RVN Airlift | 8.0% | 12.9% | 15.3% | 13.9% |

FIGURE 52

(Fig. 52--Cont'd.)          SORTIES

|  | 28-30 April | May | June | Total |
|---|---|---|---|---|
| C-7 | 213 | 2,656 | 2,363 | 5,232 |
| C-123 | 129 | 1,510 | 1,516 | 3.155 |
| C-130 | 194 | 2,326 | 1,603 | 4,123 |
| Total | 536 | 6,492 | 5,482 | 12,510 |
| All RVN Airlift | 4,472 | 35,885 | 30,496 | 70,853 |
| % of all RVN Airlift | 12.0% | 18.1% | 18.0% | 17.7% |

## HIGH PRIORITY AIRLIFT SUPPORT
### Tactical Emergency, Emergency Resupply, & Combat Essential

| High-Priority Tons | 28-30 April | May | June | Total |
|---|---|---|---|---|
| Tons | 298 | 10,443 | 4,494 | 15,235 |
| All-RVN Hi-Priority Tons | 1,748 | 12,306 | 6,127 | 20,181 |
| % of all-RVN Hi-Priority Tons | 17.0% | 84.9% | 73.3% | 75.5% |
| Avg High-Priority Tons/Day | 99.3 | 336.9 | 149.8 | 238.0 |
| Oct-Mar Avg Hi-Pri Tons/Day | 32.7 | 32.7 | 32.7 | 32.7 |
| Hi-Pri Tons as % of Tons to Aflds Supporting Cambodian Ops | 11.4% | 30.3% | 15.2% | 22.9% |

| High-Priority Sorties | 28-30 April | May | June | Total |
|---|---|---|---|---|
| Sorties | 37 | 1,510 | 491 | 2,038 |
| All-RVN Hi-Priority Sorties | 276 | 1,761 | 909 | 2,946 |
| % of all-RVN Hi-Pri Sorties | 13.4% | 85.7% | 54.0% | 69.2% |
| Avg High-Pri Sorties/Day | 12.3 | 48.7 | 16.4 | 31.8 |
| Oct-Mar Avg Hi-Pri Sorties/Day | 6.2 | 6.2 | 6.2 | 6.2 |
| Hi-Pri Sorties as % of Sorties to Aflds Supporting Cambodian Ops | 6.9% | 23.3% | 9.0% | 16.3% |

## SUPPORTING AIRFIELDS

| Airfields | Total Tons 28 April - 30 June |
|---|---|
| Song Be | 17,053 |
| Bu Dop | 12,989 |
| DJAMAP | 8,989 |
| Pleiku | 5,596 |
| Katum | 5,194 |
| Loc Ninh | 2,520 |
| Thien Ngon | 2,498 |
| Tonle Cham | 2,466 |
| Tay Ninh West | 1,709 |
| Quan Loi | 1,671 |
| Moc Hoa | 1,508 |
| Duc Co | 1,165 |
| Ha Tien South | 548 |
| Don Phuoc | 543 |
| Plei Djereng New | 404 |
| Dau Tieng | 361 |
| Chau Duc | 359 |
| Duc Lap 2 | 232 |
| Tieu Atar | 194 |
| Hon Quan | 174 |
| Thuy Dong | 158 |
| Duc Hue | 157 |
| Minh Thanh | 128 |
|  | 66,616 |

FIGURE 53

## FOOTNOTES

### FOREWORD

1. (U) Ltr, IN, PACAF to DOVD, PACAF, subj: Project CHECO Rprt, "The Cambodian Campaign, 29 Apr-30 Jun 70", 15 Aug 70.

### CHAPTER I

1. (S) Briefing, MACV J233, by Capt Charles F. Meissner, Sr Cambodian Strategic Analyst for COMUSMACV, subj: The Cambodian Situation: Background and Analysis (U), Gp-1, 12 May 70.

2. (U) Text of Address, Joint U.S. Public Affairs Office, Saigon, Vietnam, Nixon Rprt on SEA Situation, 30 Apr 70 (Wireless File).

### CHAPTER II

1. (C) JOPREP JIFFY Special Rprts 1-124, COMUSMACV.

2. (TS) Interview, Col Scott Smith, Dep Dir, TACC, 14 Jun 70.

3. (TS) Msg, C/C MACV to UCMDR, 7AF, 220404Z Apr 70;
   (TS) Msg, CJCS to COMUSMACV, 250125Z Apr 70.

4. (TS) Msg, 7AF TACC to DASCs, 281310Z Apr 70;
   (TS) Msg, 7AF TACC to Nakhon Phanom AB, 281300Z Apr 70.

5. (TS) Msg, 7AF TACC to 14th SOS, 280410Z Apr 70;
   (TS) Msg, 7AF TACC, 291045Z Apr 70;
   (C) Ltr, Brig Gen Roberts to Nguyen Dinh Lan, 30 Apr 70.

6. (C) Interview, Lt Col Robert G. Daugherty, ALO, 1st Air Div, 6 May 70. (Hereafter cited: Daugherty Interview.)

7. (C) Ibid;
   (C) Interview, Lt Col Ronald E. Bryan, ALO, TF Shoemaker, 3 May 70.

8. (C) Daugherty Interview;
   (C) Interview, Capt Michael C. Press, Head Beagle FAC, 7 May 70.

9. (C) Interview, Col Kingston, Comdr, 3d Bde, 4 May 70;
   (C) Interview, Maj Lorenzo M. Dozz, G-2, 1st Air Cav Div, 7 May 70.

10. (C)  Interview, Capt Robert C. Kimball, Air Ops FAC, and TF Shoemaker, 3 May 70;
    (C)  Interview, Capt Joseph Kopec, G-2 Air, 1st Air Cav Div, 3 May 70;
    (C)  Interview, Maj Lorenzo M. Doss, G-2, 1st Air Cav Div, 7 May 70.

11. (C)  Interview, Capt John A. Norden, Rash FAC, 3 May 70;
    (C)  Interview, Maj Don L. Brooks, Rash FAC, 3 May 70;
    (C)  Interview, Maj Robert E. Drawbaugh, Redmarker ALO, 3 May 70;
    (C)  Interview, Capt William F. Peavy, Nile FAC, 4 May 70;
    (TS) Msg, Col Scott Smith to Brig Gen John W. Roberts, 011530Z May 70.

12. (C)  Interview, Capt George N. York, S-3 Air, 3d Bde, 4 May 70;
    (C)  Interview, Capt George E. Patch, Asst S-3, 11th ACR, 4 May 70;
    (C)  Interview, Col Nguyen Van Tho, Comdr, 3d ARVN Abn Bde, 4 May 70;
    (C)  Daugherty Interview.

13. (TS) Interview, Brig Gen John W. Roberts, Dir, 7AF TACC, 6 Jun 70;
    (C)  Interview, Lt Col Bryan, ALO, TF Shoemaker, 6 May 70.

14. (S)  Notes, Maj David I. Folkman, Jr., on TF Shoemaker Planning Meeting, 2-3 May 70.

15. (C)  Interview, Capt David F. McAdoo, 3d Bde Aviation Platoon, 5 May 70;
    (C)  Interview, Capt John A. Norden, Rash FAC, 3 May 70.

16. (TS) Interview, Brig Gen John W. Roberts, Dir, 7AF TACC, by Maj David I. Folkman, Jr., and Maj Philip D. Caine, 6 Jun 70;
    (TS) Notes, Maj David I. Folkman, Jr., 4-5 May 70.

17. (C)  Interview, Capt William F. Peavy, Nile Control Duty Officer, 4 May 70.
    (C)  Interview, Door Gunners, C&C Ship, 1st Air Cav Div Arty, 5 May 70.

18. (C)  Interview, Maj Robert E. Drawbaugh, ALO, 3d ARCN Abn Bde, 3 May 70.

19. (C)  Interview Col Kingston, Comdr, 3d Bde, 5 May 70;
    (C)  Interview, Lt Col Norman H. Moffett, Comdr, 1/12 Bn, 6 May 70;
    (C)  Interview, Lt Col James L. Anderson, Comdr, 1/5 Bn, 1 May 70;
    (C)  Interview, Col Nguyen Van Tho, Comdr, 3d ARVN Abn Bde, 4 May 70.

20. (C)  Questionnaire, USAF/TACP, 2d Bde, 25th Inf Div, "Air Support in Cambodia," 22 Jun 70.

21. (C)  Response to Questionnaire, Lt Col Charles G. Maynaud, ALO, 25th ARVN Inf Div, "Air Support in Cambodia," 23 Jun 70.

22. (U)  Ltr, Lt Gen Michael S. Davison, Comdr, Air Ops, MACV, 14 Jun 70.

23. (C)  Rprt, 834th Air Div Ops, 1 Jul 70.

24. (C)  Interview, SP4 Richard O. Grubb, Sr Analyst, Cambodian Desk, MACV J-2.

25. (C)  PERINTREP Nr 21-70, II FFV;
    (C)  Briefing, Capt Arthur C. Akeman, OIC, OB Logistics, CICV, 26 Jun 70.

26. (S/NF)  Briefing, Capt Richard E. Schroeder, OIC, Out-Country Log Desk, Logistics Section, OB Branch, CICV, Impact of Current Cambodian Cross-Border Ops, Annex C, 1 Jul 70.

## CHAPTER III

1. (S)  Cambodian Intelligence Briefings, 7AF (Published Daily), 4 May - 1 Jul 70. (Hereafter cited: Cambodian Intelligence Briefing.)

2. (S)  Briefing, DI 7AF, Cambodian Situation, 18 Jun 70. (Hereafter cited: DI Briefing.)

3. (TS)  Msg, JCS to CINCPAC, Info COMUSMACV, 161713Z May 70.

4. (TS)  Msg, JCS to CINCPAC, Info COMUSMACV, 161728Z May 70.

5.       Ibid.

6. (TS)  Msg, COMUSMACV to CINCPAC, Info CJCS, 191547Z May 70.

7. (TS)  Msg, JCS to CINCPAC, Info COMUSMACV, 200008Z May 70.

8. (TS)  Msg, COMUSMACV to CINCPAC, Info CJCS, 210918Z May 70.

9. (TS)  Msg, CJCS to CINCPAC, Info COMUSMACV, 240136Z May 70.

10. (TS)  Interview, Col Malcolm E. Ryan with Majors David I. Folkman and Philip D. Caine, 7AF, 5 Jun 70. (Hereafter cited: Ryan Interview.)

11. (TS)    Msg, 7AF TACC to 504th TASG, 240452Z May 70.

12. (TS)    Msg, 7AF to 366th TFW, Da Nang AB, 251200Z May 70;
    (TS)    Msg, 7AF to 3d TFW, Bien Hoa Ab, 270845Z May 70.

13. (S)     Interview, Lt Col W. G. Ralph with Maj Philip Caine, 7AF,
            8 Jun 70.
            (Hereafter cited: Ralph Interview.)

14. (TS)    Interview, Col Scott Smith with Majors David I. Folkman
            and Philip D. Caine, 7AF, 15 Jun 70;
    (TS)    Memo of Agreement, ROE, Cambodia, 20 May 70;
    (TS)    Ryan Interview.

15. (TS)    Memo of Agreement, ROE, Cambodia, 20 May 70;
    (TS)    Ryan Interview.

16. (TS)    Ryan Interview.

17. (S)     Briefing, 7AF DITT, "Target Development Process," 1 Jun 70.
            (Hereafter cited: DITT Briefing.)

18. (TS)    Msg, JCS to CINCPAC, 202311Z May 70.

19. (TS)    Ryan Interview;
    (S)     DITT Briefing;
    (T)S    Interview with Brig Gen John W. Roberts by Majors David I.
            Folkman, and Philip D. Caine, 6 Jun 70. (Hereafter cited:
            Roberts Interview.)

20. (S)     DITT Briefing.

21. (TS)    Memo for Brig Gen John W. Roberts, subj: Intelligence
            Targeting in Cambodia, 21 May 70. (Hereafter cited:
            Roberts Memorandum.)

22. (TS)    Rprt, 7AF TACC, "Air Ops in Cambodia, 29 Apr-22 Jun 70,"
            23 Jun 70. (Hereafter cited: TACC Report.)

23. (TS)    Msg, CINCPAC to COMUSMACV, 210422Z May 70.

24. (TS)    Msg, JCS to CINCPAC, 222253Z May 70.

25. (C)     Summary, 7AF, In-Country Reconnaissance (Published Daily),
            1 Apr - 30 May 70.

26. (TS)    Msg, 7AF to 460th TRW, 261100Z May 70;
    (TS)    TACC Report.

27. (TS)    Ltr, Lt Col Bu Tith to USMACV, subj: Request and Authorization
            for Airstrikes, 29 May 70.

28. (TS)  Msg, 7AF to MACV (J-3), 301240Z May 70.
29. (S)   Ralph Interview.
30. (TS)  TACC Report.
31. (TS)  Msg, CINCPAC to CINCPACAF, 06324Z May 70.
32. (TS)  Ryan Interview.
33. (TS)  Msg, 7AF to II DASC, 091215Z Jun 70.
34. (TS)  Memo of Understanding, Brig Gen John W. Roberts, USAF: Maj Hin Nim, FANK; Maj Penn Rannda, CAF, 6 Jun 70.
35. (TS)  Msg, 7AF to 3d TFW, 110515Z Jun 70.
36. (S)   DI Briefing.
37. (TS)  Msg, COMUSMACV to Comdr, 7AF, 030755Z Jun 70;
    (TS)  TACC Report.
38. (TS)  Msg, COMUSMACV to Acting CJCS, 091210Z Jun 70.
39. (TS)  Msg, Adm Thomas H. Moorer, Acting CJCS, to Adm John S. McCain, Jr., CINCPAC, 092333Z Jun 70.
40. (TS)  TACC Report.
41. (C)   Logs, TACC, "Sorties Flown in FREEDOM DEAL," (Hereafter cited: TACC Logs.)
42. (TS)  TACC Report.
43. (C)   TACC Logs.
44. (S)   Cambodian Intelligence Briefing;
    (TS)  TACC Report.
45. (TS)  Briefing (Proposed), TACC to COMUSMACV, 15 Jun 70.
46. (TS)  Msg, Adm Thomas H. Moorer, Acting CJCS to Adm John S. McCain, Jr., CINCPAC, Gen Creighton W. Abrams, Jr., COMUSMACV, 160424Z Jun 70.
47. (TS)  Msg, JCS to CINCPAC, 172344Z Jun 70.

48. (TS)    Msg, COMUSMACV to CINCPAC, 172344Z Jun 70.
48. (TS)    Msg, COMUSMACV to CINCPAC, 181005Z Jun 70.
49. (TS)    Msg, Adm John S. McCain, Jr., to Gen Creighton W. Abrams, Jr., 190213Z Jun 70.
50. (TS)    Msg, 7AF to 23d TASS, 201145Z Jun 70;
    (TS)    Msg, 7AF to 23d TASS, 191455Z Jun 70.
51. (TS)    Msg, 7AF to III DASC, 220955Z Jun 70;
    (TS)    Interview, Lt Col Alfred C. Baker, Jr., with Maj Philip Caine, 4 Jul 70.
52. (TS)    Msg, 7AF to III DASC, 220955Z Jun 70;
    (TS)    Msg, 7AF to COMUSMACV, 250350Z Jun 70.
53. (TS)    TACC Report.
54. (S)     Msg, 7AF to CINCPACAF, 241125Z Jun 70.
55. (C)     Ltr, TACO to VNAF TACC, Coordination between VNAF and USAF, 25 Jun 70.
56. (TS)    Msg, 7AF to COMUSMACV, 250350Z Jun 70.
57. (C)     TACC Logs.
58. (S)     Cambodian Intelligence Briefings.
59. (TS)    TACC Report;
    (C)     TACC Logs.
60. (S)     Cambodian Intelligence Briefings.
61. (C)     Msg, COMUSMACV to CG, DMAC, 201037Z May 70;
    (C)     Msg, 7AF to 3d TFW, 280945Z Jun 70.
    (C)     Msg, 7AF to 3d TFW, 191015Z Jun 70;
    (C)     Interview, Capt Louis Annacone by Maj Philip Caine, 20 Jul 70.
62. (TS)    Msg, 7AF to CG, 1st MAW, 260955Z Jun 70.
63. (C)     TACC Logs.
64. (TS)    Msg, COMUSMACV to Comdr, 7AF, 290950Z Jun 70.
65. (TS)    Msg, CINCPAC to COMUSMACV, 301100Z Jun 70.

APPENDIX I

## AIR SUMMARY
## USAF

| UNIT | ACFT TYPE | PSYWAR | | FLARE DROP | | AIRB ALERT | | CBT TROOP | |
|---|---|---|---|---|---|---|---|---|---|
| S= Sorties FT=Fly Time | | S | FT | S | FT | S | FT | S | FT |
| 12SOS | C-123 | 5 | 11.5 | | | | | | |
| 834ARD | C-123 | | | | | | | 2 | 4.0 |
| 9SOS | C-123 | 1 | 2.1 | | | | | | |
| 12SOS | UC-123 | 39 | 104.1 | 11 | 42.8 | | | | |
| 315TAW | UC-123 | | | 1 | 5.3 | | | | |
| 374TAW | C-130 | 3 | 8.6 | | | | | | |
| 8TFW | C-130 | 4 | 18.6 | | | | | | |
| 834ARD | C-130 | | | | | | | 10 | 20.0 |
| 817CS | AC-47 | | | | | 1 | 3.3 | | |
| 834ARD | C-7 | | | | | | | 136 | 273.7 |
| 9SOS | C-47 | 36 | 93.8 | | | | | | |

| UNIT | ACFT TYPE | AIR ABORT | | AIR INTERDICTION | | ESCORT COVER | | RES CAP | | PHOTO RECON | | CLOSE AIR SUPPORT | | STRIKE | | FLACK SUPPRESSION | | MUDY | |
|---|---|---|---|---|---|---|---|---|---|---|---|---|---|---|---|---|---|---|---|
| S= Sorties FT=Fly Time | | S | FT | S | FT | S | FT | S | FT | S | FT | S | FT | S | FT | S | FT | S | FT |
| 12TFW | F-4 | 30 | 61.9 | 72 | 94.5 | 2 | 4.0 | | | | | 121 | 167.5 | 592 | 808.2 | | | 56 | 74.9 |
| 366TFW | F-4 | 42 | 51.3 | 277 | 432.7 | | | 2 | 3.0 | | | 117 | 376.4 | 385 | 560.5 | | | | |
| 8TFW | F-4 | 6 | 9.2 | 6 | 9.8 | | | | | | | | | 15 | 23.7 | | | | |

| UNIT | ACFT TYPE | AIR ABORT | | AIR INTERDICTION | | ESCORT COVER | | RES CAP | | PHOTO RECON | | CLOSE AIR SUPPORT | | STRIKE | | FLAK SUPPRESSION | | RUDY | |
|---|---|---|---|---|---|---|---|---|---|---|---|---|---|---|---|---|---|---|---|
| | | S | FT | S | FT | S | FT | S | FT | S | FT | S | FT | S | FT | S | FT | S | FT |
| 8TFW | A-37 | 24 | 34.1 | 142 | 212.9 | | | | | 1 | 1.9 | 1978 | 2488.6 | 58 | 74.7 | 2 | 3.7 | | |
| 3TFW | F-100 | 9 | 13.8 | 40 | 55.6 | | | | | | | 284 | 333.0 | 14 | 17.5 | | | | |
| 31TFW | F-100 | 74 | 96.4 | 272 | 389.0 | | | | | | | 853 | 1297.8 | 1047 | 1545.6 | | | | |
| 35TFW | F-100 | 30 | 33.4 | 138 | 208.2 | | | | | | | 1850 | 2713.7 | 100 | 135.2 | | | | |
| 432TRW | RF-4 | | | | | | | | | 1 | 2.8 | | | | | | | | |
| 460TRW | RF-4 | 2 | 2.6 | | | | | | | 57 | 120.3 | | | | | | | 43 | 62.4 |

| UNIT | ACFT TYPE | AIR ABORT | | AIR INTERDICTION | | ARMED RECON | | CLOSE AIR SUPPORT | | FLARE DROP | | STRIKE | | VISUAL RECON | | ESCORT COVER | | RECON ESCORT | |
|---|---|---|---|---|---|---|---|---|---|---|---|---|---|---|---|---|---|---|---|
| S=Sorties FT=Fly Time | | S | FT | S | FT | S | FT | S | FT | S | FT | S | FT | S | FT | S | FT | S | FT |
| 14SOW | AC-119 | 5 | 16.3 | 1 | 2.7 | 1 | 3.2 | 9 | 36.1 | 1 | 4.5 | | | | | | | | |
| 17SOS | AC-119 | 14 | 49.6 | 9 | 35.8 | | | 127 | 511.7 | 20 | 76.0 | | | | | | | | |
| 18SOS | AC-119 | 9 | 29.9 | 5 | 18.3 | 1 | 1.3 | 7 | 26.7 | 3 | 11.8 | | | | | | | | |
| 22SOS | A-1 | | | | | 2 | 6.8 | | | | | | | | | | | | |
| 56SOW | A-1 | 4 | 10.2 | 4 | 10.8 | 6 | 27.8 | 4 | 16.8 | | | | | | | 4 | 15.4 | 10 | 25.7 |
| 8TFW | AO-123 | 3 | 8.8 | | | 3 | 9.9 | | | | | 1 | 3.0 | | | | | | |

| UNIT | ACFT TYPE | ARMED PAC | | CLOSE AIR SUPPORT | | FWD AIR CONT | | MAINT | | TRAINING | | VISUAL RECON | | PSYCH WAR | | AIR ABORT | | AIR REFUEL | |
|---|---|---|---|---|---|---|---|---|---|---|---|---|---|---|---|---|---|---|---|
| S=Sorties FT=Fly Time | | S | FT | S | FT | S | FT | S | FT | S | FT | S | FT | S | FT | S | FT | S | FT |
| 19TAS | OV-10 | 131 | 373.8 | 5 | 15.7 | 685 | 1896.3 | 4 | 2.3 | 4 | 3.5 | 420 | 633.6 | | | | | | |
| 21TAS | OV-10 | | | | | 8 | 24.9 | | | | | | | | | | | | |
| 19TAS | O-1 | | | | | 6 | 18.9 | | | | | 8 | 29.8 | | | | | | |
| 21TAS | O-1 | | | | | 138 | 399.0 | | | | | 99 | 197.6 | | | | | | |

| UNIT | ACFT TYPE | ARMED FAC | CLOSE AIR SUPPORT | FWD AIR CONT | PAINT | TRAINING | VISUAL RECON | | PSYCH WAR | | AIR ABORT | | AIR REFUEL |
|---|---|---|---|---|---|---|---|---|---|---|---|---|---|
| 22TAS | O-1 | | | 233 590.8 | | | 353 | 616.4 | | | | | |
| 19TAS | O-2 | | | | | | | | 2 | 7.5 | | | |
| 9SOS | O-2 | | | | | | | | 2 | 9.3 | | | |
| 19TAS | O-2A | | | 95 332.1 | | | 97 | 308.9 | | | | | |
| 21TAS | O-2A | | | 129 404.5 | | | 88 | 163.9 | | | | | |
| 22TAS | O-2A | | | 44 154.9 | | | 83 | 175.6 | | | | | |
| 9SOS | O-2A | | | | | | | | 6 | 1.6 | | | |
| 19TAS | O-2B | | | | | | | | 2 | 11.5 | | | |
| 21TAS | O-2B | | | | | | | | 1 | 5.3 | | | |
| 22TAS | O-2B | | | | | | | | 1 | 3.3 | | | 1 1.5 | |
| 9SOS | O-2B | | | | | | | | 300 | 670.5 | | | |
| 23TAS | O-2B | | | | | | | | 1 | 6.1 | | | |
| 307SW | KC-135 | | | | | | | | | | | | 26 104.0 |

| UNIT | ACFT TYPE | AIR ABORT | | RADIO DIR FIND | | |
|---|---|---|---|---|---|---|
| | | S | FT | S | FT | |
| S=Sorties FT=Fly Time | | | | | | |
| 360TEW | EC-47 | 18 | 72.7 | 409 | 2549.2 | |
| 361TEW | EC-47 | 2 | 1.4 | 66 | 454.5 | |
| 362TEW | EC-47 | | | 33 | 230.8 | |

| UNIT | ACFT TYPE | PHOTO RECON | | IR RECON | | RADIO RELAY | | AIR ABORT | | VISUAL RECON | |
|---|---|---|---|---|---|---|---|---|---|---|---|
| | | S | FT | S | FT | S | FT | S | FT | S | FT |
| S=Sorties FT=Fly Time | | | | | | | | | | | |
| 460TFW | RF-4 | | | 35 | 65.2 | | | | | 99 | 198.2 |

| UNIT | ACFT TYPE | PHOTO RECON S | PHOTO RECON FT | IR RECON S | IR RECON FT | RADIO RELAY S | RADIO RELAY FT | AIR ABORT S | AIR ABORT FT | VISUAL RECON S | VISUAL RECON FT |
|---|---|---|---|---|---|---|---|---|---|---|---|
| 432TRW | RF-4C | 15 | 39.4 | | | | | | | | |
| 460TRW | RF-4C | 79 | 153.8 | 64 | 130.7 | 1 | 2.3 | 5 | 6.3 | 108 | 304.3 |
| 460TRW | RB-57 | 92 | 163.8 | 2 | 3.6 | 1 | 2.0 | | | | |
| 460TRW | RF-101 | 216 | 441.2 | 1 | 1.8 | | | 7 | 14.1 | 2 | 5.2 |

## AIR SUMMARY VNAF

| UNIT | ACFT TYPE | FWD AIR CONT S | FWD AIR CONT FT | VISUAL RECON S | VISUAL RECON FT | AIR ABORT S | AIR ABORT FT | PSYCH WAR S | PSYCH WAR FT | CLOSE AIR SUPPORT S | CLOSE AIR SUPPORT FT | AIR INTERDICTION S | AIR INTERDICTION FT | AIRB ALERT S | AIRB ALERT FT | FLARE DROP S | FLARE DROP FT |
|---|---|---|---|---|---|---|---|---|---|---|---|---|---|---|---|---|---|
| S=Sorties FT=Fly Time | | | | | | | | | | | | | | | | | |
| 112LS | O-1 | 69 | 170.6 | 40 | 68.4 | | | | | | | | | | | | |
| 114LS | O-1 | 90 | 127.1 | 34 | 60.2 | | | | | | | | | | | | |
| 116LS | O-1 | 57 | 144.3 | 86 | 190.3 | | | | | | | | | | | | |
| 112LS | U-17 | | | 3 | 5.0 | 1 | 2.5 | 49 | 80.7 | | | | | | | | |
| 114LS | U-17 | | | | | 4 | 8.8 | | | | | | | | | | |
| 116LS | U-17 | | | | | | | 46 | 126.7 | | | | | | | | |
| 514FS | A-1 | | | | | | | | | 372 | 602.4 | | | | | | |
| 518FS | A-1 | | | | | | | | | 294 | 399.4 | | | | | | |
| 520FS | A-37 | | | | | 2 | 2.6 | | | 184 | 211.1 | 4 | 5.0 | | | | |
| 524FS | A-37 | | | | | | | | | 216 | 279.1 | | | | | | |
| 817CS | AC-47 | | | | | 1 | 3.8 | | | 38 | 157.5 | | | 23 | 73.8 | 29 | 101.7 |
| 817TS | AC-47 | | | | | | | | | 5 | 45.5 | | | 1 | 2.8 | 1 | 3.9 |
| 522FS | F-5 | | | | | | | | | 199 | 166.2 | | | | | | |

APPENDIX II

USING AIRPLANES

AIRPLANES CARRYING BOMBS, NAPALM, AND 20MM CANNON ARE AVAILABLE FOR YOUR USE. YOU CAN REQUEST THESE AIRPLANES EITHER FROM PHNOM PENH OR AN AIRBORNE "FORWARD AIR CONTROLLER" (FAC) ON FM FREQUENCY 42.5. THIS WILL BE A COMMON FREQUENCY AND YOU MAY BE ASKED TO SWITCH TO ALPHA-46.80 BRAVO-59.65 CHARLIE-63.30 DELTA-63.65 ECHO-67.75 FOXTROT-69.00 (I.E. IF THE FAC SAYS "COME UP ALPHA" SWITCH YOUR PRC-25 TO 46.80). YOU MAY BE ABLE TO SPEAK TO THESE FACS IN CAMBODIAN OR FRENCH, BUT, IF ANYONE WHO SPEAKS ENGLISH IS AVAILABLE, KEEP HIM NEAR YOUR PRC-25 RADIO. TELL PHNOM PENH OR THE FAC YOUR SITUATION AND PROBLEM (I.E. CLOSE ENEMY TROOPS, TAKING MORTAR FIRE, ETC.) AND THEY WILL PROVIDE AIRPLANES IN ABOUT 45 MINUTES. KEEP TALKING TO THE FAC AT ALL TIMES, INFORMING HIM OF THE TACTICAL SITUATION. WHEN THE AIRCRAFT ARRIVE, THE PILOTS WILL DEPEND ON THE FAC TO TELL THEM WHERE TO BOMB, AND THE FAC WILL DEPEND ON YOU TO TELL HIM WHAT YOU WANT BOMBED. IF THE ENEMY IS OVER 500 METERS OR SO FROM YOUR POSITION, PICK A BIG MOUNTAIN, RIVER, FIRE, ETC., THAT BOTH YOU AND THE FAC CAN SEE AND TELL THE FAC, FOR EXAMPLE, TO HIT 700 METERS ON A HEADING OF 250° FROM THAT POINT. IF YOU ARE GOING TO BE DEFENDING A POSITION FOR A LONG PERIOD OF TIME, MAKE A LARGE, EASILY SEEN ARROW (20 FEET LONG) THAT YOU CAN PIVOT AND POINT AT THE ENEMY, AND THEN TELL THE FAC HOW FAR AWAY THE ENEMY IS. AT NIGHT, PUT OIL SOAKED RAGS IN A CAN ALONG THE ARROW AND BURN THEM. AS THE ENEMY GETS CLOSER WE WILL BE MORE INTERESTED IN YOUR POSITION THAN HIS. IF YOU HAVE SMOKE OF ANY KIND, USE IT TO IDENTIFY YOUR POSITION. IF NO SMOKE IS AVAILABLE USE PANELS MADE OUT OF RAGS, SHIRTS,

BLANKETS, ETC., AND LAY THEM ON THE GROUND PARALLEL TO YOUR POSITION. THEN TELL THE FAC WHERE YOU ARE FROM THESE PANELS (IE NORTH OR SOUTHWEST ETC.). ONCE THE FAC KNOWS WHAT YOU WANT BOMBED, HE WILL MARK THAT POSITION FOR THE AIRPLANES TO HIT WITH HIS SMOKE. THE STRIKE WILL FOLLOW IMMEDIATELY. ANOTHER WAY TO IDENTIFY A POSITION TO BE STRUCK IS TO MARK IT WITH ARTILLERY OR MORTAR FIRE. KEEP YOUR PEOPLE WELL PROTECTED BY BEING IN BUNKERS, HOLES OR JUST LYING DOWN WHILE THESE PLACES ARE BEING BOMBED. ALSO KEEP THE FAC AS WELL INFORMED AS POSSIBLE ON YOUR PRESENT SITUATION AND WHERE YOU WANT THE NEXT BOMBS. THE FAC IS YOUR KEY TO GOOD AIR SUPPORT.

IF YOU HAVE A REQUIREMENT FOR AIR YOU KNOW ABOUT MORE THAN 24 HOURS IN ADVANCE, PASS THIS ALONG TO PHNOM PENH OR THE FAC AND THEY WILL SCHEDULE IT FOR YOU. THIS WILL GIVE US TIME TO SET UP THE AIRCRAFT AND THE CREWS.

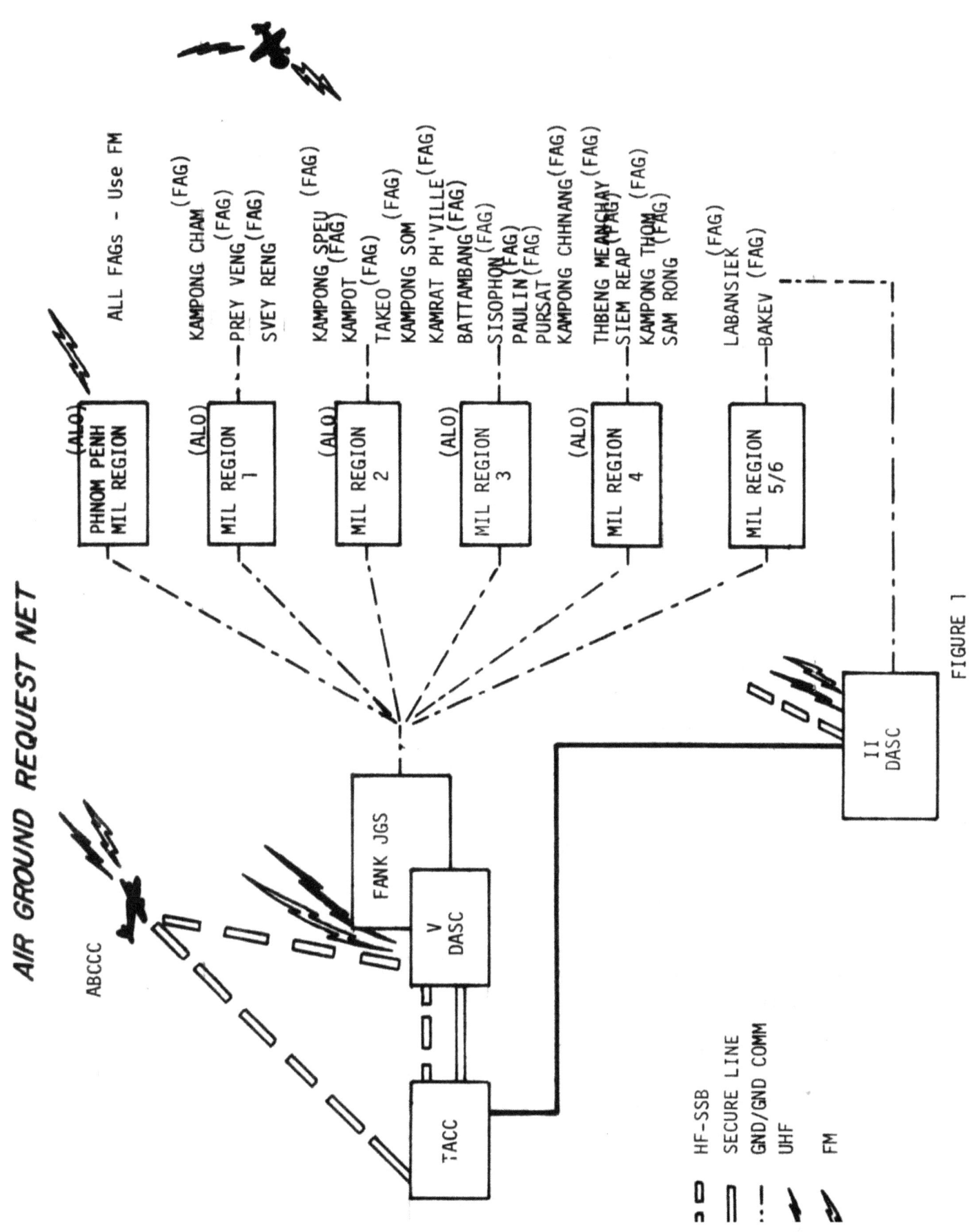

FIGURE 1

## USE OF SIGNAL PANELS

1. Panels should also be used to mark the position of friendly patrols or other small units that do not have radios. The same panels cannot be used all the time or the enemy may learn of them and use the same panels to mark their positions. The following panel schedule is suggested to mark positions of friendly units that do not have radios:

| Date | Panel |
|---|---|
| 25 June 70 | L |
| 26 June 70 | T |
| 27 June 70 | A |
| 28 June 70 | ▭ |
| 29 June 70 | X |
| 30 June 70 | V |
| 1 July 70 | ▭ |
| 2 July 70 | L |
| 3 July 70 | V |
| 4 July 70 | X |
| 5 July 70 | L |
| 6 July 70 | ▭ |
| 7 July 70 | T |
| 8 July 70 | A |
| 9 July 70 | X |
| 10 July 70 | V |

2. In addition to marking and validating the position of friendly forces without radios, panels can be used to indicate direction and distance to enemy forces. The suggested method is as follows:

    a. An arrow to indicate direction:

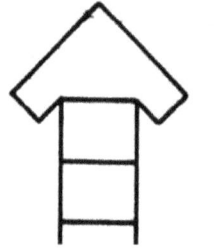

b. Short Distances indicated by 100 meter panels paralleled to the arrow as follows:

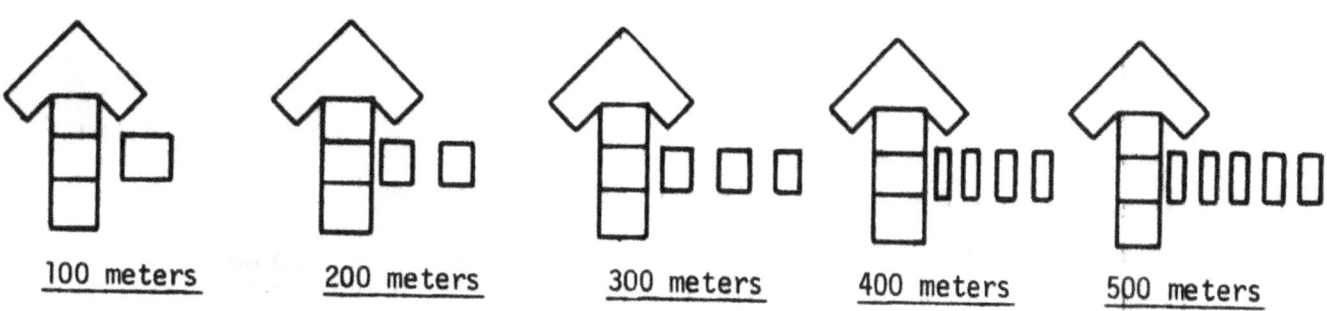

c. Longer distances (500 meters +) indicated by combination 500 meter and 100 meter panels. The 500 Meter panels are placed 90 degrees to the arrow, the 100 meter panels are placed paralleled to the panels. Examples follow:

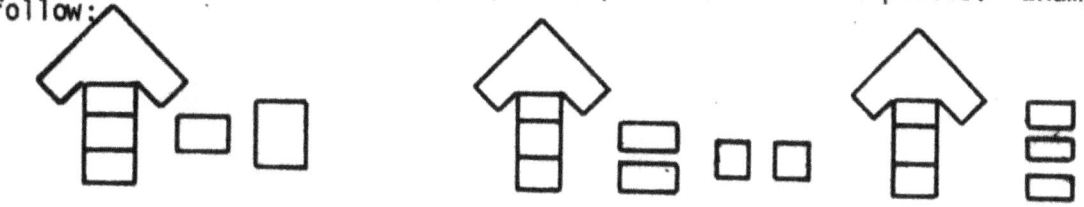

## APPENDIX III

## FREEDOM DEAL LOC STATUS

At the time of the inauguration of the interdiction campaign in northeast Cambodia, the condition of the primary LOCs and their suitability for interdiction varied. Of the primary waterways, the Mekong River from the Laos Border south to Kratie was navigable for motorized watercraft as was Waterway 4 from Southern Laos to Stung Treng and Waterway 6 from Stung Treng east to the RVN border. Waterway 7 was navigable only by small craft from Stung Treng east to the RVN border.

The major north-south road was Route 13, which paralleled the Mekong from the Laotian border south to Kratie, and then turned to Snuol and the RVN border. The road was generally in good to excellent condition and a portion of it from Stung Treng to near Kratie was asphalt and concrete. There were 16 bridges and a ferry crossing the rivers along this route. The major eastwest route in the interdiction area was Route 19, which extended from Stung Treng to the RVN border. It was in generally good condition although not hard-surfaced. Route 194 was motorable southeast from the Laotian border to its junction with Route 19 at Bung Long; and Route 141 was motorable to just south of Lomphat, where it became a trail. Route 133 connected Routes 13 and 141 across the southern portion of the area and was motorable but in poor condition. Route 97 from the Laotian border south to Siem Pang was in trail status and portions of it were overgrown.

## GLOSSARY

| | |
|---|---|
| ACR | Armored Cavalry Regiment |
| ALO | Air Liaison Officer |
| AO | Area of Operation |
| ARDF | Airborne Radio Direction Finding |
| ARVN | Army of Republic of Vietnam |
| ABCCC | Airborne Battlefield Command and Control Center |
| Abn | Airborne |
| | |
| BDA | Bomb Damage Assessment |
| Bde | Brigade |
| | |
| Cav | Cavalry |
| CBU | Cluster Bomb Unit |
| CJCS | The Chairman, Joint Chiefs of Staff |
| CMD | Capital Military District |
| COMUSMACV | Commander, U.S. Military Assistance Command, Vietnam |
| COSVN | Central Office of South Vietnam (VC Hq) |
| | |
| DASC | Direct Air Support Center |
| | |
| FAC | Forward Air Controller |
| FANK | National Forces of Cambodia |
| FARK | Rpyal Forces of Cambodia |
| FFV | Field Forces Vietnam |
| FM | Frequency Modulation |
| | |
| GOC | Government of Cambodia |
| GVN | Government of Vietnam |
| | |
| HF | High Frequency |
| HLZ | Helicopter Landing Zone |
| | |
| IDP | Interdiction Point |
| IR | Infrared |
| | |
| JGS | Joint General Staff (Vietnamese High Command) |
| | |
| KBA | Killed by Air |
| KHMER | Ethnic Cambodian |
| KHMER Rouge | Cambodian Communists |
| KIA | Killed in Action |
| | |
| LOH | Light Observation Helicopter |
| LRRP | Long-Range Reconnaissance Patrol |
| LZ | Landing Zone |
| | |
| MACV | Military Assistance Command, Vietnam |
| Medevac | Medical Evacuation |

| | |
|---|---|
| NVA | North Vietnamese Army |
| OpRep | Operations Report |
| POL | Petroleum, Oil, and Lubricants |
| PSYWAR | Psychological Warfare |
| PW | Prisoner of War |
| ROE | Rules of Engagement |
| RTAFB | Royal Thai Air Force Base |
| RVN | Republic of Vietnam |
| RVNAF | Republic of Vietnam Armed Forces |
| SAR | Search and Rescue |
| SECDEF | Secretary of Defense |
| SLAR | Side-Looking Airborne Radar |
| TACC | Tactical Air Control Center |
| TACP | Tactical Air Control Party |
| TIC | Troops in Contact |
| TOC | Tactical Operations Center |
| TOT | Time over Target |
| UHF | Ultra High Frequency |
| USN | United States Navy |
| VNAF | Vietnam Air Force |

www.ingramcontent.com/pod-product-compliance
Lightning Source LLC
Chambersburg PA
CBHW080546170426
43195CB00016B/2694